Comparative Frontiers

Comparative Frontiers:
A Proposal
for Studying
the American West

by

Jerome O. Steffen

University of Oklahoma Press : Norman

by Jerome O. Steffen

William Clark: Jeffersonian Man on the Frontier (Norman, 1977)
The Frontier: Comparative Studies (co-editor) (Norman, 1977)
The American West: New Perspectives, New Dimensions (editor)
  (Norman, 1979)
Comparative Frontiers: A Proposal for Studying the American West
  (Norman, 1980)

Library of Congress Cataloging in Publication Data

Steffen, Jerome O   1942–
  Comparative frontiers, a proposal for studying the American West.

  Bibliography: p.
  Includes index.
  1. Frontier and pioneer life—The West—Historiography.   2. The
West—Historiography.   3. Frontier and pioneer life—The West.
4. The West—History.
I. Title.
F596.S827   978'.007'2   79–20315
ISBN 0–8061–1617–X

For Lewis E. Atherton
Inspiring teacher and friend

Contents

Preface

This book is an attempt to generate a larger approach to western history. While I present my ideas in a direct manner, they are meant only to be suggestions. This book is not meant to be dogmatic but rather undertakes to bring relevant generalizations before the scholarly community. It is highly speculative and based on selective documentation. Its value, therefore, will lie in the amount of critical discussion it generates. The main focus is on comparative American frontier change and continuity and the historical processes involved in producing each of these conditions. The frontier was a natural laboratory for this approach because it represented a stage of historical development usually associated with the new and unknown, providing an actual or conceived test for established notions and practices that people brought to it.

The analysis of change in any historical context involves disassembling the many woven threads that produce historical development. This is a difficult job at best because the relationships among the threads fluctuate or vary in relation to each other. For my purposes frontier variables fall into two broad categories: those inherent in the demands of the frontier environment and those associated with prefrontier experiences. Frontier change and frontier continuity were both contests between the demands of the environment and the mindset of those entering the confines of the situation. The relationship between the two components was determined by how compelling and obvious environmental demands were for change and how deeply rooted were prefrontier principles and practices.[1]

This approach is not meant to be a rigid examination of man's adaptation to differing environments such as cultural ecologists in geography and anthropology employ. Such an emphasis is generally inadequate for the historian. Few historians study history in a time frame broad enough to allow the evolutionary contest between man and environment to work out completely. For example, Great Plains agriculture is viewed as a victory of technology over an otherwise hostile environment. But since this phenomenon is only approximately one hundred years old, man's so-called victory may represent only a dysfunctional stage of adaptation.

The historian interested in frontier change must be aware not only of the rate of change but also of the kinds of change. Some changes in American history may represent fundamental alterations in human thinking; others are modal in nature. For example, the ideological alteration in American history up to the nineteenth century certainly cannot be considered in the same context as the adaptation of agricultural techniques to the Great Plains of North America. In comparing American frontiers, it is necessary to be aware of different levels of change. Change may be classified as either modal or fundamental. Modal change usually represented an altered overt manifestation of a practice or belief whose conceptual foundation remained essentially the same. Fundamental change involved the replacement or significant alteration of the very assumption upon which given practices were based.

Given these suppositions, the comparative study of American frontier development could help determine not only what variables or combinations of variables caused different kinds of change but whether the variables were intrinsic or extrinsic to the frontier environment. I am suggesting that there is a direct relation between the degree of insularity and the level of change experienced on any given frontier. Insularity, in turn, can be determined by analyzing the nature and number of interacting links between a given frontier and its parent culture. If the interacting links were few in number or nonexistent, the frontier was insulated to a significant degree from its parent culture, a condition that increased the importance of the indigenous environment as a causative factor for change. Therefore, frontiers with inherent environments that called for change and with few interacting links were more likely to experience fundamental change. And, of course, the reverse was true for those frontiers that possessed many interacting links with their parent cultures.

Interacting links are associated with questions that western scholars easily recognize. The most obvious relate to the level of technology and its ability to connect frontier regions with the main body of "civilization." This factor is related to other links associated with key economic questions. Was economic activity specialized or nonspecialized? Did local or national and international economic conditions determine economic success? Time might also constitute an interacting link. For an individual exposed to frontier conditions for only brief periods of time, memory served as an interacting link, because the connection between the frontiersman and his problem-solving reference base was not severed. Once the interacting links have been clearly defined and outlined, the scholar then needs to juxtapose them to the frontier environment with an eye toward how compelling its demands were for change.

In this hypothesis, American frontier experiences fell into two broad categories, cosmopolitan and insular. Cosmopolitan frontiers were associated only with modal change or change caused by factors not found exclusively within the confines of the frontier. Insular frontiers were associated with fundamental change caused primarily by factors exclusive to the frontier experience. In this hypothesis trans-Appalachian agricultural settlement was the only insular frontier in American historical development, because the number of interacting links between it and the main body of American civilization were few in number. Diverse and, for brief periods, self-sufficient economic practices characterized it. During its nonmarket-oriented pioneer stage, the frontiersmen had to rely on themselves rather than on outside factors for success. The presence of only a few interacting links highly insulated this frontier,

producing a stronger interaction between the frontiersman and his environment. The end result was pervasive
and fundamental change.

Western historians have tended to use Turner's ideas
rigidly, viewing the frontier experience as the sole cause
of the pervasive changes associated with American history up to the early nineteenth century. Their instincts
may have been correct, but the focus was wrong. By
narrowly concentrating on pioneer agricultural settlement, they missed the point that this frontier experience
was a mere part of a larger frontier process. That process involved more dimensions than agriculture and
related to more than the geographical boundaries of
the United States. The trans-Appalachian agricultural
frontier experience did cause some fundamental changes
but also was a subfrontier developing simultaneously
within a larger process: America as an insular frontier
of Europe.

The lack of fundamental economic, political, and
social change characterized cosmopolitan frontiers.
Many of the factors that served as interacting links in
the trans-Appalachian agricultural frontier were absent
in the fur-trading, ranching, and mining frontiers. As
a result they possessed a low degree of insulation from
the main body of American civilization and consequently experienced little indigenous development and
truly fundamental change.

Fur trading, for example, did not involve any fundamental changes from previous practices and attitudes
already well established when first brought to the New
World from Europe. This is true in general of the Amer-

ican and European trading establishments as they related to the national and imperial designs of their respective countries. A comparative view of environmental problems both European and American traders faced shows how similar business practices in each country reflected similar solutions to these problems. Finally, the diversity of nationalities on the fur-trading frontier presents an interesting laboratory for determining if diversity became homogeneity, as Turner held, as a result of shared frontier experiences. If they were not visibly changed because of their frontier experiences, an explanation for the lack of change is in order.

The ranching frontier represented another example of a cosmopolitan frontier, which experienced little fundamental change. The ranching frontier will be examined in terms of its interaction with national affairs, its business practices, and the impact of the frontier environment on individuals associated with it. The high number of interacting links in this frontier experience did not allow the degree of insulation and hence the degree of indigenous development necessary to cause fundamental change.

Early cattlemen came to the western ranges not as community organizers but as financial venturers and economic empire builders. The inherent demands of the ranching environment in the initial years did not discourage already well-established mercantile-capitalist practices. Many of the pioneers in Texas cattle had previous trading histories, and their experience as cattle traders did not change this entrepreneurial behavior pattern. The careers of these cattlemen when compared with each other and with individuals on the other cosmopolitan frontiers can help illustrate the relationship between interacting links, degrees of insulation, degrees of indigenous development, and the levels of change.

The mining frontier, like ranching and fur-trading frontiers, can be classified as cosmopolitan because it too possessed many characteristics that served as interacting links. Economic specialization, geographic mobility, and technological advances all linked it to the main body of American civilization. Miners more than any other frontier dwellers depended on others for goods and services. More than any other frontiersmen they were linked to national political, economic, and social development. The careers of claims promoters and locators, for example, involved orientation to eastern capital and the vagaries of the national and international monetary situation.

The pursuit of precious metals in camp and boomtown settings prevented all but the most temporary commitment to local affairs. When it did, national trends or memory of how things were done previously generally dictated people's actions. Like cattlemen and fur traders, did prospectors, claims promoters, and locators share economic and social behavioral patterns? Did their frontier experiences affect previously learned behavior? A prosopographic review shows a pattern of continuity in their behavior, albeit amplified in cases where individuals suddenly became wealthy. All these factors, when combined, linked the mining frontier to national development in many ways, never allowing the high degree of indigenous development necessary for fundamental change.

Apparently democratic tendencies in the mining frontier, such as vigilante justice, *de facto* governments, and mining codes, may not have been born on the mining frontier, but were brought to it from the outside. These developments reflected national trends rather than a unique mining-frontier experience.

Considering the conceptual foundations upon which economic, political, and social structures rest, Great Plains agricultural settlement offered little that is fundamentally new. This settlement may not even fall within the parameters of frontier studies. It is true that life-supporting techniques were adapted to meet semi-arid conditions, and Walter Prescott Webb, in *The Great Plains* covered them very well. Farming techniques, barbed-wire fencing, and windmills were modal adaptations, not fundamental changes. The Plains settlers' economic, political, and social views, already shaped, were transplanted to the Plains, where they essentially remained intact or changed with national currents.

Given this view of the settlement of the Plains, why did fundamental change cease? Great Plains settlement, from the start, was not insulated. Technological advances such as the railroad and the telegraph served to prevent the degree of insulation earlier eastern agricultural settlers had experienced. There was little need to adapt to environmental conditions because technological advances overcame the obstacles and perpetuated established practices. Plains settlers were part of the national economy, and were rapidly incorporated into the national culture.

Great Plains agricultural settlement along with the corporate stages of mining and ranching, then, were merely western extensions of national development and need to be studied from that perspective. The relevance of nonfrontier western settlement lies in the ability of western historians to relate otherwise provincial studies to broader national themes. Western attitudes toward such matters as urban development, industrialization, and labor movements generally corresponded to national attitudes.

There is one major exception to this contention, and that is western mythology. Mountain Men, cowboys, prospectors, and other western characters have become a significant and unique part of American popular culture. This arena of western study is extremely significant, though it falls outside this study.

In summary, American frontier development fell into two settlement experiences: cosmopolitan and insular. Early ranching, fur trading, and the placer stage of mining were all frontiers that shared similar historical components cosmopolitan in nature. They were short term and economically specialized. National and international affairs determined success there. As a result there was a lack of insulation from national developments and no commitment to indigenous development. Thus no fundamental alteration in economic, political, and social institutions and behavior patterns followed. When change did occur on these frontiers, factors extrinsic to their environments were the cause.

Eastern agricultural settlement, on the other hand,

possessed a contrasting set of frontier variables that were insular in nature. This frontier was long term and economically diverse. Immediate surroundings, not national or international economic conditions, determined success. Eastern agriculture in its pioneer stage experienced a high degree of insulation and a consequent commitment to indigenous development, increasing the chances for discernible fundamental change to occur.

Undertaking a study such as I have just outlined is at best perilous, but it is necessary because the western scholarly community has become for all practical purposes a closed society. With some notable exceptions communications between western historians and the American historical profession in general have been minimal. It is hoped that this book can make a small contribution toward the reestablishment of this communication network. We can begin by recognizing that the ingredients of the western historical process were not fundamentally different from those associated with historical processes of other times and places. Second, we must recognize that individuals associated with the American West, like all others, functioned as problem solvers who attempted to gain maximum political and economic success while maintaining intellectual and social stability. Finally, we must recognize that the physical and social environment that surrounded westerners determined in large part the range of their problem-solving capacities.

This book owes its existence to many individuals whose patient council and assistance I cannot stress too much. My indebtedness extends to David Murrah and Ms. Tommie Whiteley, of the Southwest Collection at Texas Tech University, and to Archibald Hanna and his staff, of the Western Americana Collection at Yale University. I also wish to thank Gene M. Gressley, Howard Lamar, and H. Wayne Morgan for comments and criticisms that prevented me from making errors. I am responsible for any that may remain, however. I am also deeply indebted to Ms. Mary Roland and Ms. Martha Penisten, who typed the manuscript and whose ability to decipher all-but-illegible handwriting borders on genius. The University of Oklahoma provided me the research funds to complete the study. Special thanks go to Lewis E. Atherton, to whom this book is dedicated. Professor Atherton provided the initial inspiration and many of the perspectives contained in this work. I hope that, in some small way, it measures up to the standards of this great man. Finally, there is my wife, Gloria Roth Steffen, whose support and encouragement are a continual source of amazement.

JEROME O. STEFFEN

Comparative Frontiers

CHAPTER 1

Cis-Mississippi Pioneer Agricultural Settlement: A Subfrontier Process

The cis-Mississippi farming frontier unfolded during a period when America experienced some of its most fundamental political, economic, social, and intellectual changes. Most scholars are familiar with Frederick Jackson Turner's attempt to connect the two developments. In Turner's view, "The existence of an area of free land, its continuous recession and the advance of American settlement explain American development."[1] According to Turner:

American democracy was born of no theorists' dream; it was not carried in the Susan Constant to Virginia, nor in the Mayflower to Plymouth. It came out of the American forest, and it gained new strength each time it touched a new frontier. Not the constitution but free land and an abundance of natural resources open to a fit people, made the democratic type of society of America for three centuries while it occupied its empire.[2]

To Turner the presence of free land attracted individuals of varying backgrounds and nationalities to the frontier. The isolation encountered on the frontier both prompted the erosion of the traditional and promoted the growth of new practices and ideas produced by the diverse mixture of individuals who shared the frontier experience. The frontier also served as a safety valve or an avenue of escape for society's malcontents and so affected America's more developed areas.

With the maturation of America as an industrial state the days of Turner's frontier hypothesis were numbered. A distinguished Turner scholar, Ray Allen Billington, put it thus:

An interpretation of the American past that stressed agrarianism rather than industrialism, rugged individualism rather than state planning, and optimistic nationalism rather than political internationalism seemed outmoded in a one-world of machines and cities suddenly beset by bewildering economic cataclysm.[3]

Most scholars are familiar with the attacks on the Turner thesis, which centered mainly on its vagueness and gross generalizations. There is no need to review these criticisms yet again.

In 1951, Walter Prescott Webb's *The Great Frontier* readdressed American historical development in terms of the frontier, but from a much broader perspective.[4] Webb hypothesized that the discovery of the New World threw the social and economic structures of Europe into a state of disarray. The presence of so many natural resources created less emphasis on land and more on goods or "things." "Things," then, became the basis for a thriving capitalistic structure, which increasingly placed a lower priority on the landed aristocracy and more on the producer or manufacturer of "things."

4

This phenomenon was reflected in a trend of the central government to relegate more freedom and responsibility to the individual because it could afford to do so. According to Webb, this trend reversed itself after the Great Depression of the 1930s, when the government began to take back many of the responsibilities relegated to the individual in an earlier age. This cycle was essentially a frontier phenomenon in which the New World represented a four-hundred-year boom period.[5]

Webb, like Turner, never clearly or precisely explained how the individual forces which comprised American history came together to foster these changes; but like Turner, Webb, too, was instinctively getting at some very important matters. He sensed that, in addition to specific frontier experiences, America was part of an international frontier process. In another writing, Webb more clearly examined this phenomenon:

This minute examination of the many little frontiers, little "Easts" and little "Wests," has resulted in the accumulation of a wealth of data about the processes that went on and has revealed a small central core of uniformity. The invasion of the little "West," the area of free land, has always had some effect on the little "East," on the civilization of that particular fragment.

The next step is to assemble all the little "Wests," all the fragments of the frontier, into the whole frontier, the greater "West," and when we have done this, we have a greater frontier than we have previously been examining; we have the whole instead of a parcel of parts of which the United States is only one. This whole Great Frontier originally would have comprised the three and one-half continents and the thousands of islands opened up by Columbus and his associates. This is a synthesis that was inevitable and is logical, once the idea of frontier has been accepted as a force in history.[6]

In 1966, with the publication of *America's Frontier Heritage,* Ray Allen Billington recast the Turner thesis in more modern terms. Billington set out to test the thesis by using a more precise methodology. He clarified much of Turner's terminology and qualified many of his broader contentions. Billington, for example, made a clearer distinction between the frontier as a place and as a process, defining the former as

a geographical region adjacent to the unsettled portions of the continent in which a low man-land ratio and unusually abundant, unexploited, natural resources provide an exceptional opportunity for social and economic betterment to the small-propertied individual.[7]

The frontier functioned as a process because

socio-economic experiences and standards of individuals were altered by an environment where a low land-man ratio and the presence of untapped natural resources provided unusual opportunities for individual self-advancement.[8]

This altered definition did not diminish the central importance of the frontier in American development. Although Billington found that the frontier was not an innovative catalytic agent, it did serve as an adaptive agent and as an amplifier of institutions and characteristics inherited from the Old World.

Lest Billington and Webb be criticized for prolonging an anachronistic thesis, it should be pointed out that Turner's hypothesis, in a rudimentary and perhaps unwitting manner, anticipated some of the concerns of present-day social scientists. Turner's assumption that frontier environments dominated the frontiersmen, though oversimplified and too deterministic, is the essential foundation of cultural ecology, an interest which holds a significant place in modern anthropology and geography.[9] Furthermore, it would not be stretching a point to say that Turner instinctively and unwittingly anticipated the work of social psychologists influenced by Freud and of those sociologists who stress the importance of role playing.

Of the social psychologists the most significant to the frontier specialist are Abram Kardiner, Erich Fromm, and Erik Erikson, whose work applied Freud's theories of individual behavior to whole societies. Freud was of course interested in finding universal laws of psychic development. He concentrated on the tension created between desired sexual objects and cultural trappings instilled in individuals from childhood which tended to act as obstacles to the fulfillment of these natural desires. Kardiner and Fromm, while still adhering to the importance of childhood learning experiences, looked not only to universal laws of individual psychic development but to similarities possessed by given societies in child-rearing practices and how these similarities then collectively affected the cultural development of certain societies.[10] These studies, then, have direct historical application because collective cultural pressures and individual learning act upon each other to produce historical direction.

If Fromm's and Kardiner's interests are juxtaposed to Erik Erikson's, the usefulness of these studies to the historian, particularly the frontier historian, becomes quite obvious.[11] After all what could be more central to the frontier scholar than the tensions produced between learned behavior and new environments? Erikson sees this process at work in producing American civilization, a civilization that is characterized by the challenge of new environments to existing practices and beliefs. The result produced what Erikson termed an identity crisis, a crisis that begins the search for truth. The crisis, and the search, according to Erikson, is

easily misunderstood, and often it is only dimly perceived by the individual himself, because youth, always set to grasp both diversity in principle and principle in diversity, must often test extremes before settling on a considered course. These extremes, particularly in times of ideological confusion and widespread marginality of identity, may include not only rebellious but also deviant, delinquent, and self-destructive tendencies."[12]

Erikson's statement invites application to all of American history, a history of expansion and growth and consequent change of environmental needs and cultural pressures; hence, a constant "identity crisis." To Erikson this search manifested itself in extremely opposing traits, pitting individuals against the pressures of collec-

8

tive behavior in political, economic, and, especially, religious affairs. For example, one might contrast the Christian notion of a suffering pilgrimage on earth to the actual abundant conditions of the New World. The contrast between the reality of the New World and previous conceptual structures caused the shift in theological thinking manifested in American Protestantism.

To a scrutinizing eye Turner's hypothesis indeed has some bearing on the work of Fromm, Kardiner, and Erikson. Turner's reference to the "perennial rebirth" caused by the moving frontier seems to describe the constant shift in environments and social pressures apparent in what Erikson called an "identity crisis." To Turner the advancing frontier was more than a line but a process of rebirth in which social development was constantly beginning over again. Does not the statement, "continually beginning over again," whether correctly or incorrectly perceived by Turner, have some relevance to Fromm's socialization process in which individuals learn to conform to society in order to effectively deal with its problems and challenges?

It also might be said that Turner's work is not that far removed from the much-discussed work of sociologist David Riesman. In *The Lonely Crowd,* Riesman combined role-playing concepts with the social psychological emphasis of Fromm.[13] Role-playing studies emphasize categories of behavior—based on age, sex, class, or occupation—which individual societies assess and by which members are acculturated into their societies. They learn roles much as actors or actresses do. Individuals contribute something of themselves to the assigned role so that subtle nuances may emerge within the stereotypes. Persons interested in becoming doctors must learn how doctors behave (role playing). Yet they bring their own personalities to that role in subtle ways (individual psychological development). Working from this premise, Riesman contends that American character has undergone and is still undergoing a tremendous change from "inner directed" to "other directed." To Riesman inner direction is a characteristic of preindustrial civilization, one in which the individual is socialized in an "authoritative family group by impressive and often oppressive parents." Riesman sees these people as being gyroscopically steered:

The parent installs a gyroscope in them and it stabilizes them all their life. . . . Theirs is a world in which the opening frontiers are the frontiers of production, discovery, science . . . a society in which people are very much aware and interested in the malleability of the physical environment, the organizational environment, and in their social mobility, their ambitions.[14]

Riesman metaphorically depicts the other-directed individual as possessing a mental radar used to interpret the signals sent by his social surroundings. Consequently this individual "is oriented very early in life, not to his ancestors, not to his parents or to his image of their exalted selves, but to his peers." In other words present social conditions, not tradition, socialize the individual. "For him the frontiers are not the frontiers of production but the frontiers of consumption, the frontiers of much more abundant leisure and consumer goods. . . .

10

And he looks to others for guidance as to whether he is experiencing the right experiences on the frontiers of consumption."[15] Turner's hypothesis, stressing the breakdown of tradition on the frontier, seems to have some correlation to Riesman's gyroscopic adaptations in a changing world.

If the frontier scholar is uncomfortable in the realm of the anthropologist, social psychologist, or sociologist, he might return to the more familiar ground represented by the myriad of nineteenth-century European travel accounts of American life. Reading these accounts, one continues to be tempted to draw an association between frontier development and the major departure American history took from that of Europe.[16]

The most balanced and insightful of these accounts is Alexis de Tocqueville's *Democracy in America*. For the purposes of this inquiry his most striking observation points to the irony in the development of an individualistic American mind and its contradictory social and political implications:

When the inhabitant of a democratic country compares himself individually with all those about him, he feels with pride that he is the equal of any one of them; but when he comes to survey the totality of his fellows and to please himself in contrast with so huge a body, he is instantly overwhelmed by the sense of his own insignificance and weakness. The same equality that renders him independent of each of his fellow citizens, taken severally, exposes him alone and unprotected to the influence of the greater number. The public, therefore, among a democratic people, has a singular power, which aristocratic nations cannot conceive; for it does not persuade others to its beliefs, but it imposes them and makes them permeate the thinking of everyone by a sort of enormous pressure of the mind of all upon the individual intelligence.[17]

Accounts such as Tocqueville's not only provide a beginning rationale for seeing an association between the frontier and American development, they also serve as a bridge between early observations and those of contemporary behavioral scholars. If one views the significance of collective societal pressures as seen in Fromm, Erikson, and Riesman, how do they differ so much from Tocqueville's observations on the "tyranny of the majority," and the collective "pressure of the mind of all upon the individual intelligence"?

Despite efforts to suggest a latent sophistication in Turner's frontier hypothesis, it still remains a statement of faith, based on intuition. It is easily susceptible to criticism. Indeed the chapters that follow in this book will attempt to demonstrate that the Turnerian frontier process did not function in the fur-trading, ranching, and mining frontiers. There is a basis however for considering Turner's propositions in the study of the cis-Mississippi agricultural frontier if a more empirical application can be found.

Stanley Elkins and Eric McKitrick have partly penetrated this methodological roadblock. Elkins and McKitrick set out to study political democracy in the Old Northwest using methods that three sociologists—Robert K. Merton, Patricia S. West, and Marie Jahoda—first employed in their study of two public-housing communities, Hilltown and Craftown. Both communities were under the control of the Federal Public Housing Authority, and both were homogenously populated. Hilltown and Craftown differed in one important respect. The latter was beset with myriad problems, including shoddy construction, lack of public utilities, no public transportation, and inadequate police protection. The problems confronting Craftown "were so overwhelming, so immediate, so pressing, that the residents could not afford to wait upon the government for action. They were therefore forced to behave in that same pattern which so fascinated Tocqueville: they were driven to the forming of associations."[18] Community meetings were held and committees established out of which grew a flurry of activity which resulted in a volunteer fire and police department, a local legal structure and, among other things, a cooperative store. Craftown, in "times of trouble," produced a situation where "persons who had previously never needed to be concerned with politics now found themselves developing a familiarity with institutions, acquiring a sense of personal competence to manipulate them, to make things happen, to make a difference." They went on to say that, "with many offices to be filled, large numbers of people found themselves contending for them; the prestige connected with officeholding, the sense of energy and power involved in decision-making, became for the first time a possibility, a reality, an exploitable form of self expression."[19] The structure of Hilltown, on the other hand, "proved quite adequate for the handling of Hilltown's concerns, it was never seriously challenged, and it required no supplementation by resident activity. 'Democracy,' in short was unnecessary there."[20]

This sociological town-model study, according to Elkins and McKitrick, had direct application to frontier community development because "periods of wholesale migration to the West forced a setting in which such an experience (Craftown) as that just outlined had to be enacted a thousand times over. Frederick Jackson Turner has stated the undeniable fact—that an organic connection exists between American democracy and the American frontier."[21]

Certainly Elkins and McKitrick bear out Turner's contentions and move one step further in offering a methodology by which to categorize and isolate frontier components with an eye toward the development of political democracy. Their work has the attraction of isolating two variables, conflict and harmony, as causative factors for the furtherance of political democracy. Whether or not their findings are correct, they at least present a typology amenable to more objective analysis. It is now necessary to expand on Elkins and McKitrick's work to include a complex of variables along with a hypothetical model to explain how they interacted in given situations to produce given results.

Still remaining, however, is an explanation of the relationship between cis-Mississippi agricultural settlement and the array of methodological devices presented so far in this chapter. To begin: all the macrointerpretations of the development of American character presented so far concern the individual's interaction with his immediate environment, and his ability—determined by the outcome of this interaction—to rearrange or adapt his life in order to successfully negotiate a world that had changed during his lifetime. Working from this common bond, frontier scholars might find it useful to view this interaction as it related to American historical development up through the first half of the nineteenth century.

When frontier historians of this period attempt to confine this interaction to frontier situations, they have been rightfully criticized for being at best monocausationist and at worst provincial. That is because they have too narrowly concentrated on pioneer agricultural settlement. Consequently they have missed the essential perspective which sees pioneer agricultural settlement as part of a larger frontier process, a process more dimensional than agricultural and more dimensional than the geographical boundaries of the United States. Therefore, while the cis-Mississippi agricultural frontier experience did serve as a cause of fundamental change, it was perhaps a subfrontier acting simultaneously within the parameters of a larger frontier process, namely America as a frontier of Europe, first suggested by Walter Prescott Webb.

Western scholars therefore might find it useful to review existing nonfrontier studies in American history up to the mid-nineteenth century from the perspective of the frontier model of change and continuity presented in this volume. For example, the decline of a citizenry deferent to the ruling class manifested in many themes in American historical development, has a common causative factor, and that causative factor might be found in a "Great Frontier" perspective.

To illustrate this point, one might begin by reviewing the work of the colonial demographers, especially that of Kenneth Lockridge on Dedham, Massachusetts, which demonstrates how significant alteration in Puritan secular development eventually was reflected in a fundamental theological change. For example, Lockridge discusses the relationship between out-migration from the community and the decline of deference to the elite in town meetings. This alteration in the political structure of Dedham eventually made itself felt in the religious structure, such as the development of the half-way covenant.[22] It does not take much historical imagination to see the relationship between Puritan out-migration and the analysis of frontier environments.

This same theme is central to the study of the revolutionary period and especially to the work of Bernard Bailyn and Gordon Wood. Bailyn and Wood contrast the fundamental ideological reorientations of colonial America on the eve of the War of Independence with more superficial economic and political changes. Bailyn, in his discussion of the relationship between the Enlightenment and the Revolution, suggested that it amounted to "a fundamental revision of early American history." The Enlightenment, according to Bailyn,

did not create new social and political forces in America. They released those that had long existed, and vastly increased their power. This completion, this rationalization, this symbolization, this lifting into consciousness and endowing with high moral purpose inchoate, confused ele-

16

ments of social and political change—this was the American Revolution.[23]

Two aspects of this "completion" and "realization" were the increased citizen participation in decision making and the fear of the unruly masses that this participation caused in older elitist circles. Gordon Wood, in his monumental study *The Creation of the American Republic, 1776–1787,* pointed out that

the most pronounced social effect of the Revolution was not harmony or stability but the sudden appearance of new men everywhere in politics and business. "When the pot boils, the scum will rise," James Otis had warned in 1776; but few Revolutionary leaders had realized just how much it would rise.[24]

It seems reasonable to carry Bailyn and Wood's work into studies of the New World frontier environment with its interacting links between the colonies and the mother country and its consequent effect on the difference between actual and apparent historical reality.

The decline of the deferential citizenry becomes more obvious as the scholar moves into nineteenth-century American history. John William Ward's *Andrew Jackson: Symbol for an Age* is perhaps the most useful study for illustrating this theme because it presents a generalized picture of Jackson's symbolic significance and how it represented, if only in imagery, the commonality of American thinking.[25] Ward discusses the "anti-traditional experience" as seen in such concepts as Nature, Providence, and Will and how it

17

nourished the "idea that every man has the making
of his own greatness within his own determination."[26]
The *Illinois Gazette,* in 1825, illustrated this trend toward increasing confidence in the masses and in common sense as a vehicle for wise and intelligent decision
making. The *Gazette* noted that Jackson was

> endowed with the facilities to see the whole and grasp the
> most remote relations of vast and comprehensive designs,
> he is the most qualified to govern. We should blush, if we
> could say with truth that he would make a good secretary of
> the Treasury, of the Navy, of State or of the Post Office. We
> hope and believe that he would not; We hope that he is
> above such works, incompetent he cannot be. But for the
> great designs he is fashioned by nature, and therefore would
> he advance the general interest and glory of the republic,
> beyond any other man.[27]

The *Gazette's* endorsement also implies that fundamental changes in education had occurred by the early
nineteenth century. The association of formal training
with pedantry and the affirmation of individual genius
were common ingredients in new conceptions of education that openly rejected traditional or European
standards of education for more immediate and practical training. There was less emphasis on great literature, philosophy, natural history, and natural science
—all ingredients of a classical education. Denial of the
utility of a classical education was not an endorsement
of antiintellectualism. It merely represented a change
in the premise upon which wisdom was obtained. From
this new perspective truth and wisdom were not beyond

18

the reach of any citizen who desired them. The common man need not defer to an elite corps of the educated.[28]

The evolution of American religion represented another manifestation of the "decline of the deferential citizenry." Fundamental American theological changes began crystallizing in the Great Awakening of the 1740s. The changes generally represented a shift from reason to emotion and from debates on the nature of God to debates on the nature of man and his capacity to receive salvation. The science of a rational age and the mysticism of earlier Christianity inevitably were headed for a clash, and the Great Awakening represented the working out of these differences in the New World. Alan Heimert, a noted scholar of American religion, says of this development: ". . . the Awakening, by shattering the communities and the social assumptions inherited from the seventeenth century, allowed the evangelical ministry to offer the American people new commitments, political as well as ethical."[29]

American Protestantism emerged from the Great Awakening in the form it would maintain throughout the nineteenth century. The proliferation of sects and the theological debates were mostly superficial manifestations of the conceptual differences crystallized in the Great Awakening. Philip Schaff, a German theologian visiting the United States in the mid-nineteenth century, was keenly aware of this phenomenon: "I proceed now to consider the several confessions—'denominations' they are called in America, because the difference is in fact often merely nominal and relates not so much to the doctrinal confession, as to government, worship, and outward usage."[30]

Nor did the fundamental change in the theological premise of American Protestantism escape Schaff, whose first intentions were to help stamp out the proliferation of sects because of their pantheistic tendencies. Schaff instead returned to Germany and endorsed the New World religious events as the religion of the future. He saw American Protestantism as a melting pot of "all the powers of Europe, good and bad . . . fermenting together under new and peculiar conditions."[31] The fermentation of the good and bad aspects of Europe under "new and peculiar conditions" represents a historical dynamic common to all aspects of early American development, a development that represented a fundamental change from the old order. Frontier scholars may wish to view this phenomenon in terms of the New World frontier environment and its impact on the secularization of American life—specifically its impact on destroying interacting links between the fonts of religious truth and actual frontier religious practices.

The development of the individualistic set of mind is clearly represented in American constitutional and legal history. James Willard Hurst, in *Law and the Conditions of Freedom in the Nineteenth Century United States,* convincingly describes these changes in nineteenth-century constitutional concepts. Hurst asserts that there were three premises which served as the foundation of nineteenth-century law: first, man is creative; second, liberty is necessary for man's creativity to flourish; and third, the relationship between the two has special significance because of the natural abundance of the United States.[32] These principles were manifested in the shortening of tenure of office for local judges, suggesting an accommodation to a citizenry confident in its ability to write and interpret its own laws. The sudden and frequent practice of overturning long-established court rulings in local courts was just another indication of this trend.

It was the restructuring of incorporation procedures, however, that was the most telling indicator of the depth of change in nineteenth-century law. They were streamlined to make incorporation strictly a private matter, eliminating the need for government consent that had seemed restrictive and harmful to individual advancement and national growth.[33]

The historical literature of the Jacksonian period in general, in dealing with such topics as the rise of free banking, the rise of the "small capitalist," the nature of political parties and national policies, clearly demonstrates the same decline in the deferential citizenry.[34] In succinct fashion Stuart Weems Bruchey, the noted economic historian, ties together these diffuse topics when he suggests that the economic character brought to the New World possessed a "quality of alertness to the possibility of material betterment," and that

with the progressively greater market opportunities provided by both government and private business during the late eighteenth and early nineteenth centuries, it seems increasingly to have permeated the American people. It is tempting to put a special emphasis upon the importance of this pro-

21

gressive permeation, this wide diffusion of the demand for growth. Because of it the "dynamic, innovative activities" productive of revolution in transport, agriculture, and industry were, to cite the language of John E. Sawyer, "sustained by great numbers of people." We became a "nation of projectors," not a mere "handful of enlightened families or officials or banks, or a scattering of Schumpeterian heroes," but a "population swarming with actual and potential entrepreneurs in all walks of life—multiple centers of initiative, able and motivated to respond, and . . . even to overrespond to the stimuli of the market and of expanding opportunity."[35]

Whether early American development is viewed politically, economically, or socially, there are grounds for viewing it in terms of the frontier process, a process in which the pressures for change exerted by the New World environment are juxtaposed to the number of interacting links in existence between America and its Western European reference base. The interaction of the two forces constitutes a large and complex frontier process, a process which contains many subfrontiers represented by the themes just reviewed. It is in this context that the cis-Mississippi agricultural frontier must be viewed: a subfrontier of a larger frontier, nothing more, nothing less. Consequently, the causative burden for the profound changes in many aspects of American history must not rest with the American agricultural frontier experience. Nor can Webb's suggestion for a broader view of the frontier stand without further elucidation.

It is this thought that has influenced my attempt to establish a model by which frontiers can be analyzed

22

universally in the context of the historical components they share with other frontier experiences. Applied specifically to the hypothesis I am suggesting, the frontier specialist would begin by categorizing the numbers and kinds of interacting links that were operational between the mother country and the New World and at the same time by juxtaposing these links to a New World environment that compelled change. It seems that this starting point would give the frontier specialist a clear picture of those areas where the colonists were more insulated from the mother country and the environment more demanding of change. The inquiry, then, could proceed to determine if those areas where few interacting links existed—that were therefore more insulated from the Old World and so more susceptible to indigenous development—actually experienced more fundamental change than other areas where more interacting links were operative.

This method of analysis, when applied specifically to cis-Mississippi agricultural settlement, would search for those variables that indicate the degree of insulation and consequent level of indigenous development. The agricultural frontier is synonymous with self-sufficiency or with that stage of agricultural development when the settler was family-oriented in determining his needs for future crop production. Self-sufficiency, of course, was not self-imposed but rather was determined by the high cost of transporting goods (because of the initial lack of internal improvements). Furthermore, the pioneer agriculturalist usually was concerned initially with establishing a capital base by clearing land to improve

23

the value of his property and by constructing the necessary implements to make his operation more efficient. Energies expended on these activities could not therefore be used to produce goods for a market, even if one were available.

Another variable associated with frontier agriculture was the scarcity of labor and consequentially its high cost. The family had to act as its own labor complex, using as many of its members as possible. Two English agricultural speculators came to Illinois in the early nineteenth century with hopes of establishing a large-scale farming operation complete with large numbers of hired laborers. Unable to satisfy their labor needs, they next turned to importing laborers, but in both cases they lost the services of these individuals, who were soon able to make enough money to enter into farming on their own. One English traveler in Illinois speculated that a laborer who was diligent in saving his wages could earn enough in two years to buy a quarter section of land along with some livestock and enough implements to begin operations.[36] The two speculators eventually abandoned their enterprise as they originally had conceived it.[37]

With the expansion of internal improvements for distribution, the market displaced the family for determining the quantities and types of crops to be grown. It was at this point that the agriculturalist ceased to be a part of a subfrontier process and entered upon a larger frontier process affecting the nation as a whole. The evolution of commercial agriculture and the erosion of the frontier stage of food production was an uneven process, advancing faster in some regions than in others. Percy Bidwell and John Falconer, two of the early and still important historians of American agriculture, suggest that eastern Appalachian agriculture had reached the commercial stage by 1830 while the western regions did not develop commercial agriculture until 1850.

Isolating self-sufficiency and the high cost of labor as two important agricultural frontier variables is nothing new, of course. In fact these are basic components of Turner's hypothesis. If, however, one were to use these two variables along with social, political, and intellectual variables in the context of their insulation from the parent culture, a more precise understanding of the frontier process would be gained. Employing just one variable, self-sufficiency, one could think in terms of the number of interacting links that this condition prevented.

For example, national economic programs that affected agriculture had little immediate or direct bearing on the pioneer agriculturalist. Agricultural societies, county fairs, and other institutions for disseminating new agricultural techniques, well developed in the East, had little growth in the trans-Appalachian West by the early nineteenth century. Even in the East, where agriculture had become more commercially based, self-sufficient conceptions of farming lingered. As late as 1821 the New York Board of Agriculture, the supposed seat of enlightened agricultural practices, advised the farmer to "produce everything necessary to sustain life in a comfortable and respectable manner: and he should surround himself with everything that he wants by his own industry," adding:

> It must be considered as an established principle in domestic economy that every farmer should look to his farm for all that his farm can furnish him. Though it may seem better to sell his wool and buy his bread, yet in all such cases he pays a double commission, to the purchaser of the wool and the seller of the bread, who must both get their living out of the operation.[38]

It was twenty years before that body would realistically advise the farmer of the specialized economic characteristics of commercial agriculture.

On the federal level, the House of Representatives in 1820 and the Senate in 1825 established permanent committees on agriculture. The federal government largely confined its role to adjusting tariffs and gathering and reporting statistics that affected farmers. The national impact, such as it was, affected the pioneer agriculturalist little because his surplus sales were minimal and his economic decisions were directed by the needs of his family or, at best, a local economic picture.[39]

One can easily gain a wrong impression of the amount of settlement that occurred in the trans-Appalachian West up to the mid-nineteenth century. Land speculators, and on some occasions guides to emigrants, would have one believe that the Middle West was a beehive of activity producing startling growth figures. Even one of the more responsible guides put out by

John Peck fostered this impression. After listing population statistics for Missouri, Arkansas, and Indiana, Peck concluded that "the advancement in business and improvements has been equal to the increase of population." He went on to state that "this region of country will continue to advance in the production of property, equal to its progress in numbers."[40]

Falconer suggests another perspective:

> The total population living west of Ohio was only slightly greater than the population of that state. The population of Ohio was only three-fifths that of New York State. The total area of improved land in farms in the territory of Indiana, Illinois, Michigan, Wisconsin, Iowa and Minnesota was only slightly greater than that of New York State alone. While a few small areas, such as that around Cincinnati and in the Bluegrass region of Kentucky, had a well-developed agriculture by 1840, the farming west of the Alleghenies was distinctly of the pioneer type, characterized by limited markets and capital, abundant land, and the absence of intensive farming.[41]

More detailed demographic information should be gathered and juxtaposed to other variables that might serve as interacting links between frontier regions and the main body of civilization. This would seem to open vast opportunities for employing existing data to a better understanding of the internal functioning of an insular frontier process, a process vaguely described by Frederick Jackson Turner in 1893. In the end, the frontier specialist may conclude that pioneer agriculture served as a catalyst in a frontier process begun with the first arrival of the Europeans in the New World.

Caroline Kirkland noted some remarkable changes between her residence in Michigan in 1835 and her native New York. They may have been the result of the subfrontier process which served to foster change within change. "The state of things appalled me at first; but I have learned a better philosophy since." She said of her domestic help, "I find no difficulty now in getting such help as I require, and but little in retaining it as long as I wish, though there is always a desire of making an occasional display of independence." She noted: "Since living with one for wages is considered by common consent a favor I take it as a favor; and, this point conceded, all goes well. Perhaps I have been peculiarly fortunate; but certainly with one or two exceptions, I have little or nothing to complain of on this essential point of domestic comfort."[42] Kirkland's general observations on differences between Michigan and New York are much in the same vein as Tocqueville's comments on the difference between Europe and America. This, it seems, illustrates the dual frontier process. If New York had changed from Europe, so had Michigan changed from New York.

CHAPTER 2

American Fur-trading Frontier:
New World Mercantilism

From the perspective of the insular-cosmopolitan frontier hypothesis—and compared to trans-Appalachian
agriculture—the American fur trade seems to represent
a frontier that experienced little fundamental change
from its European antecedents. This continuity is clear
from three perspectives. First, a comparative macro-
view of European and American trading establishments
shows that they similarly related to the national imperial designs of their countries. Second, a comparative
view of European and American traders reveals that
similar environmental problems spawned similar business structures as solutions to these problems. Finally,
a selective study of the fur-trading frontier in terms of
its causative effects on patterns of individual behavior
indicates that the frontier did little to homogenize diverse frontier types as Turner's thesis suggests.

American fur trading was part of the commercial
revolution and national mercantilism prominent from
the fourteenth to the eighteenth centuries. The ideology
of mercantilism launched the trader as a vital factor
in the history of rising central states and the accom-
panying struggle for world empires. Global struggles

placed severe strain on national treasuries. The individual mercantile-capitalist's economic goals were exceedingly compatible with those of the nation-state that sought greater self-sufficiency through the accumulation of bullion in an orderly colonial trade network.

From the perspective of national policy makers, the needs of individual traders and the nation-state were best served by the elimination of wasteful competition in the private sector of the economy. As a result, mercantilism on a national scale placed a premium on trade regulation in order to eliminate harmful competition within a nation's own trading community.[1] Hence the merchant trader had a symbiotic relationship with the nation-state. The nation-state offered the mercantile capitalist order and regulation through grants of monopoly and military protection wherever feasible. The mercantile-capitalist assisted the nation-state by exploring potential imperial acquisitions and directly, or in some cases unwittingly, assisting in their colonization.[2]

The American fur-trading establishment was as much a part of the national empire-building milieu as its European counterparts and consequently faced many of the same environmental obstacles. American policy makers and the trading fraternity initially faced these problems in much the same manner. The United States as an emerging nation had to face the realities of survival in an international community of nations. As with any European power this depended upon the harmonious relationship between domestic economic components and successful competition for empires. American policy makers emerging from a colonial status within the

British mercantile scheme applied the same formula for its maintenance and survival. The notion of an American mercantilism is certainly reinforced by Benjamin Franklin's description of George Rogers Clark's contribution to the fledgling American republic as a result of his efforts in securing the Old Northwest during the War of Independence. Franklin said to Clark, "Young man, you have given an empire to the Republic."[3] Further emphasizing this point, William Appleman Williams boldly asserts that "the central characteristic of American history from 1763 to 1828 was in fact the development and maturation of an American mercantilism . . . Having matured in an age of empires as part of an empire, the colonists naturally saw themselves in the same light once they joined issue with the mother country."[4]

With its national boundaries ill defined until well into the nineteenth century, the New World was the individual merchant's staging ground for potentially high profits as well as for high risk ventures. It was also the arena for potential imperial expansion. The role of the American fur trader in the trans-Mississippi West after the Louisiana Purchase in 1803 supports this notion. After the initial exploration of the Louisiana Purchase, the Far Northwest became a competitive trading ground between the United States and Great Britain. This provoked an all-out economic war in which nations competed for empires and traders competed for individual wealth, each serving the other's purpose. Mercantilist-inspired imperial designs were even on the minds of the initial explorers Lewis and Clark. Shortly after arriving on the Pacific Coast, William Clark wrote to his brother, "I consider this tract across the continent of immense advantage to the fur trade, as all the furs collected in 9/10 parts of the most valuable fur country in America may be conveyed to the mouth of the Columbia and shiped [*sic*] thence to the East Indies by the 1 of August in each year and will of course reach Canton earlyer than the furs which are annually exported from Montreal in Great Britain."[5]

If the trader was a soldier in this North American imperial struggle, then mercantilist policy, to conform to the Old World, was dictated order through monopolistic grants and regulations. As her efforts to eliminate competition among her traders clearly demonstrates, Britain followed these policies to the letter. As late as 1820, when the Hudson's Bay Company and the North West Company—two of Great Britain's most powerful soldiers in the war for imperial acquisition—began to consume each other, efforts were made to consolidate the two into one giant company which then had a complete monopoly in the Far Northwest.[6]

Unlike Britain's, the American response to the challenge of imperial acquisition in the Far Northwest was not classic mercantilism. But it was inspired by mercantilism. The American response was not classical mercantilism for three simple reasons: first, American colonial possessions were adjacent to areas already incorporated in the nation as states; second, and as a result, certain considerations had to be given to the interests of permanent settlers; and finally, if eventual permanent settlement was going to take place, the native inhabitants of the land in question had to be dealt with. This last factor was not a concern of the British, since traders only minimally disturbed the regional eco-system between peoples and environments.

Thomas Jefferson's Indian and colonial policies perhaps best illustrate how American national policy hoped to serve the goals both of imperial acquisition and permanent settlement. In neo-classical mercantilist fashion Jefferson, fearing the harmful effects of private traders, attempted to revive the factory system and extend it all the way to the Pacific Coast. Jefferson's intention to expand the factory system was prompted both by the domestic pressures of permanent settlement and by the imperial contest with Great Britain.[7] The goal, then, was simply to maintain the allegiance of the native inhabitants with an eye toward creating stability and security in American colonial possessions.

This line of reasoning contradicted another strain of Jeffersonian thought concerned with Indian assimilation. There were two Jeffersonian Indian policies. Jefferson viewed the Indian as a member, like himself, of the universal body of man and as part of the Great Chain of Being. The crucial difference in the development of different civilizations lay in the environmental forces shaping them; if this were true, then civilizations could be altered merely by changing the environmental forces acting upon them. Operating from this Enlightenment logic Jefferson concluded "that the proofs of genius given by the Indians of N. America, place them on a level with Whites in the same uncultivated state." More specifically he concluded, "As to their bodily

strength, their manners rendering it disgraceful to labour, those muscles employed in labour will be weaker
with them than with the European labourer; but those
which are exerted in the chase and those faculties which
are employed in the tracing of an enemy or a wild beast,
in contriving ambuscades for him, and in carrying them
through their execution, are much stronger than with
us, because they are more exercised." Therefore, Jefferson concluded, "I believe the Indian then to be in
body and mind equal to the white man."[8]

Jefferson reasonably assumed that Indian assimilation
would occur if the environmental forces acting upon
them could be altered. The new environment, consisting of small agricultural plots, would create a yeoman
mentality and a sense of property ownership. At this
juncture Jefferson's commercial views meshed with his
plans for Indian assimilation: the factory system would
serve as a commercial tool to bring the Indian under
American influence and in some cases would even
cause them to sell their lands as payment for incurred
debts.[9]

In the Far West beyond the immediate reach of
American settlement Jeffersonian Indian policy was not
immediately concerned with Indian assimilation. It was
instead more concerned with and responsive to the
pressures of imperial acquisition. In the near vicinity
of American settlements the factory system was to be
maintained, and strict trading regulations were to be
applied to private traders. In the Far Northwest it became increasingly apparent that the British North West
Company, before the merger with the Hudson's Bay

Company in 1821, was dominating the area and winning the allegiance of the native inhabitants. It was apparent to Jefferson that American traders—operating under his original restrictions—could never compete with such a large organization. Jefferson had two alternatives. He could have followed the suggestion of Meriwether Lewis that a large government-owned trading company be established to compete with the British, or he could simply remove all restrictions on traders operating in that region. Jefferson chose the latter.

As originally stated, American Indian and colonial policy, unlike that of Great Britain, was not a classic model of mercantilism; however, although it did not grant monopolies, it constantly stressed regulation. The harmful effects of cut-throat competition in the American trading establishment became a matter of concern to national policy makers and implementers alike. William Clark, a long-time Jefferson associate attuned to the conceptual foundations of Jeffersonian programs, reflected these fears as late as 1831 when he suggested that the Americans adapt British measures to control American traders. He referred to British trading policy as "rather despotic, yet Salutary."[10] In another proposal Clark actually counseled the establishment of a government-sponsored company with monopolistic control over trade in the Far West. He reasoned that such an organization would provide better goods for the Indian and at the same time benefit the national economy. It would also eliminate harmful competition and bring the fur trade "more under the control and management of the Government."[11]

Although Jefferson's plan to extend the factory system and Clark's pleas for a large government trading company never materialized, they revealed thinking that is consistent with a mercantilistic framework. But before such programs could be carried out, or for that matter even before additional mercantilist-inspired programs could be conceived, the dynamics of American history had made them anachronistic.

The form and structure of the American fur-trading establishment originated in earlier European business practices. American fur-trading methods, albeit on a smaller scale and in some cases at a more primitive stage, began where the great joint-stock ventures of Europe ended. The Missouri Fur Company, the American Fur Company, and countless other partnerships and joint-stock agreements were structural extensions of such famous European trading associations as the Dutch East India and English East India companies, the Virginia Company of London, and the Muscovy Company.

The structural continuity between American and European trading organizations existed no doubt because both faced similar economic environments. The major obstacles to successful trading in both hemispheres were waste and inefficiency in organization and the high risk of loss from unforeseen "acts of God" or theft and piracy. European traders met the high-risk problem through the use of the regulated company and the joint-stock association. The joint-stock company represented a pooling of capital and investors to assemble necessary funds to carry off a costly business venture; it was also a method of distributing the losses if the venture did not succeed. The usual practice was for businessmen to issue shares of stock to the public, retaining the controlling number of shares for themselves. Theoretically, once the venture was completed the association was to be dissolved, with the profits and money acquired from the sale of the company's assets divided among the shareholders.[12] The joint-stock association was the primary business structure for traders during the period of exploration and discovery, just as it was the primary structure for its counterparts in the New World, the American fur-trading community.

Mercantile capitalists were the key figures in national and individual economic aspiration during the Age of Discovery. They were sedentary merchants who sought to control their economic fortunes through diversification of function and efficient administration. Ideally they wanted simultaneous command of the full range of activities connected with a trading transaction—wholesaling, retailing, banking, warehousing, and transportation. Unlike his predecessor, the mercantile capitalist did not travel about but concentrated on efficient administration of all these variables from one set place of operation. How skillfully he used managerial skills to coordinate any army of clerks, craftsmen, laborers, ships' captains, and sailors determined his success. Control was the permanent factor in effective decision making because it determined how successful the mercantile capitalist would be in his efforts to coordinate the many variables in a given mercantile operation.[13] As in Europe, these factors were prominent in the American fur-trading business structure.

The formation of the Missouri Fur Company illustrated the similarities between European and American traders and their business structures. The Missouri Fur Company owed its existence to a shrewd entrepreneur named Manuel Lisa, who came to St. Louis in 1798 and in three years managed to become one of the city's leading traders. His efforts in the immediate surroundings of St. Louis, although successful, could not be compared to the imagined riches that lay further up the river. For this reason he needed capital and someone to share the risk of such a venture. Initially he joined in a partnership with two established Illinois merchants, William Morrison and Pierre Menard. The Lisa, Morrison, and Menard venture was the first organized venture of the Upper Missouri River.[14]

Jefferson's removal of trading restrictions in the Far Northwest spurred this partnership to seek additional capital investment for a more ambitious joint-stock arrangement. The Missouri Fur Company was the result of this goal. Its members were Benjamin Wilkinson, Pierre Chouteau, Sr., Manuel Lisa, Auguste Chouteau, Jr., Reuben Lewis, William Clark, Sylvestre Labbadie, Pierre Menard, William Morrison, and Andrew Henry.

The structure of the Missouri Fur Company was a classic example of an Old World joint-stock venture. The articles of agreement called for every member to share equally in the expenses of the fur-trading expedition. Each member was prohibited from trading sepa-

rately for individual profit. No merchandise was to be
purchased without the consent of the majority of the
partners. Certain members were given managerial powers to sign legal documents and carry out business transactions on behalf of the company. After the furs were
sent downriver and sold, profits were to be divided
equally. The association operated under a three-year
term after which all property was to be divided equally
among the members.[15]

Powerful competition from the North West Company
prevented the Missouri Fur Company from realizing
its conceived profit potential. Therefore, in 1812, the
members met to reorganize the company in hopes of
gaining more capital for a larger operation. The Missouri Fur Company now had a president and a three-
man board of directors. The new company was to have
a capital stock of not more than $50,000, with $23,000
to be sold as public shares at $1,000 each. An annual
stockholders meeting would declare dividends and
make needed changes subject to the approval of two-
thirds of the stockholders. As in a classic joint-stock
structure, managerial personnel were salaried and not
necessarily partners or shareholders of the venture. The
reorganized Missouri Fur Company sent just one expedition into the Far West, with only moderate success,
before the War of 1812 interrupted the organization's
future.[16] At their annual meeting in 1813 the members
voted to dissolve the company. Even though its last
venture netted almost $50,000 worth of furs and buffalo
robes, unstable relations with the British discouraged
all but the most diligent of traders.

After relations between the United States and Great Britain stabilized, Lisa once again had notions of returning to the Far Northwest to establish large-scale trading operations. To do so he again needed to assemble large amounts of capital, and so in 1819 the Missouri Fur Company was reorganized with a new roster of investors. The new members were Thomas Hempstead, Joshua Pilcher, Joseph Perkins, Andrew Woods, Moses Carson, John B. Zenoni, Andrew Drips, and Robert Jones. A year later Lisa died, but the company continued under the direction of Joshua Pilcher and later became known in some circles as Pilcher and Company. Pilcher continued trade on the Missouri River and made a few expeditions into the Rockies before his retirement from the fur trade in 1830. For all practical purposes, however, the Missouri Fur Company ceased to be a factor in the economic war against the British when it withdrew from the Upper Missouri River in 1813 and dissolved the organization as it was then structured.[17]

The method of capital accumulation and risk distribution associated with the life of the Missouri Fur Company was well established in Old World trading circles. Its history contained the classic symbiotic relationship between the individual mercantilist and national imperial designs.

The frame of reference for this final inquiry into the fur-trading frontier will be that of the frontier as a process; specifically a process that from the perspective of the Turner thesis promoted homogenization among the diverse collection of traders assembled and exposed to its environment. Implicit in the Turner thesis is the notion that individuals adapt uniformly to similar environmental pressures. This is a dangerous implication, but cultural ecologists of today are still fond of Turner because they share this premise. Indeed, depending on the topic of study, this approach has certain merits. In the Far West watercraft evolved to suit the environmental demands of its shallow rivers. The rendezvous system was an adaptation of Indian technology to the central Rockies environment. But does the same methodology explain the impact of the frontier on intangible concerns like intellectual patterns and social behavior? This dangerous but rewarding area needs to be explored in the future.

Only slightly less dangerous is the attempt here to analyze the impact of the fur-trading frontier environment on change and continuity in entrepreneurial behavior patterns. In other words, did the fur-trading frontier significantly alter the established entrepreneurial behavior patterns that were introduced to it? If it did not, an explanation for the continuity in behavior is needed. To illustrate, five individuals from the Pacific Fur Company will be prosopographically reviewed. These sketches are not meant to be definitive but only to serve as examples of how scholars might profitably pursue the frontier as a cause for change or continuity.

John Jacob Astor founded the Pacific Fur Company in 1811 with the full encouragement of Thomas Jefferson, in yet another example of the symbiotic relationship between the mercantile capitalist and the empire-building nation-state. In his attempt to build an international trade Astor wanted to establish a network of trading posts on the Upper Missouri to link New York with the West Coast, and also with the Far East. The War of 1812 ended the project, causing Astor to sell the venture to the British in 1813.[18] The lives of important individuals associated with this venture, Ramsey Crooks, Robert McClellan, Wilson Price Hunt, Donald McKenzie, and Robert Stuart, illustrate the larger process in microcosm.[19]

Ramsey Crooks was born in Scotland before migrating to Montreal, where he became a clerk in a mercantile trading operation in the Niagara Falls region. Crooks' duties as a clerk carried him to St. Louis where he got to know Robert McClellan with whom he formed a trading partnership in 1807. McClellan, a native Pennsylvanian, happened to be in St. Louis because of his assignment with the Army Quartermaster Corps. McClellan had been a hunter and trapper in the East before engaging in a trading venture that carried him to New Orleans. That venture failed, and McClellan returned to his home in Philadelphia and entered the employ of the army. The Crooks-McClellan partnership lasted only three years, but their careers as entrepreneurs carried them to Michilimackinac to consult with John Jacob Astor about a large trading venture he was planning. In 1810 both men became partners in the Pacific Fur Company. McClellan stayed in the association only two years before returning to Missouri to run a mercantile establishment for the remainder of his life. Crooks stayed in the fur business much longer than McClellan. In 1813 he was reassigned to the Michilimackinac region to recover furs then stored in British-held territory. Crooks moved up in Astor's organization, steadily gaining a larger portion of shares and receiving a higher salary. When Astor retired in 1834 Crooks purchased the Northern Department of the American Fur Company. The decline of fur trading and the depression of 1837 caused Crooks to retreat from the western fur fields to New York to trade on a local level until his death.[20]

Wilson Price Hunt, a New Jersey native, was already a seasoned trader when he joined the Pacific Fur Company. Hunt was engaged in a mercantile partnership for five years before he became a junior partner of Astor's. He made the initial trek to Astoria, and it was to be his last long-distance venture on the North American continent. After Astoria was sold to the British, Hunt gathered enough goods to make one profitable trading junket to the Far East before returning to St. Louis, where he remained a local merchant until his death.[21]

Donald McKenzie, Scottish by birth, migrated to Canada at age seventeen and entered the employ of the North West Company. As a New York agent of this association he caught Astor's eye, who later managed to entice McKenzie into joining the Pacific Fur Company. After the sale of the Pacific Fur Company, he returned to the North West Company. To some traders fur-trading ventures provided the capital needed to invest in more secure enterprises. For McKenzie, the fur trade became a political windfall; in 1825 he assumed the post of Governor of the British Red River

Colony. After his retirement McKenzie did not stay in the frontier environs, choosing to return to New York to live out his remaining days.[22]

Robert Stuart, also of Scottish birth, migrated to Canada to live with an uncle who, as an employee of the North West Company, introduced the young immigrant to the fur business. Stuart was one of the first members of Astor's Astoria venture, and he remained with the Astor organization after the British takeover of the Pacific operation. Stuart was reassigned as second in charge under Crooks in the Great Lakes Division of the American Fur Company. He did not remain in the employ of the American Fur Company because he was not satisfied with his advancement. He spotted a lucrative real estate enterprise in Detroit that was his concern until death.[23]

These sketches merely illustrate a technique for studying the fur frontier as a causative process for frontier change or continuity. These five traders were similar in that the fur-trading environment did not alter their entrepreneurial behavioral patterns. All five fit the classic trader-swapper stereotype, seeking windfalls even in a high-risk venture such as the Pacific Fur Company. Most demonstrated an unwillingness to remain mere employees of the association.

McClellan dropped out of the Pacific Fur Company to invest in his own mercantile establishment in Missouri. Crooks remained because of the upward mobility that eventually allowed him to purchase an entire department of the American Fur Company. In true entrepreneurial fashion Crooks returned to New York with his gains when the boom period ended to trade in a less speculative manner. Hunt also followed the entrepreneurial pattern of investing in a one-time venture with hopes of making windfall profits for investment elsewhere. Once successful, he left the high-risk sector of trading to return to local trading in St. Louis. McKenzie demonstrated much the same pattern, except that the interrelationship of individual and governmental designs were more clear in his career. McKenzie, as a result of his mercantile excursions, rose to a high political position in British colonial administration. He no doubt considered himself more of a public servant in the wilderness than an architect of civilization since he chose to live in New York after his career as a trader and government servant had ended. Stuart—like Hunt, Crooks, and McClellan—entered the trade as a partner in a high-risk, high-profit venture and, like the others who departed with their gains, moved to Detroit to invest in a real estate operation.

If western scholars agreed on the plausibility of continuity between prefrontier and postfrontier entrepreneurial behavior patterns, they would discount Turner and create a new problem: the causative elements in frontier continuity. The close links between fur traders and their parent cultures may provide a clue for these continuative patterns of behavior. In the case of the fur-trading frontier, memory might serve as the most important interacting link because traders were not long removed from the parent cultures that served as their reference bases. McClellan remained with the Pacific Fur Company for only two years before returning to Missouri to live out his days as a storekeeper in Cape Girardeau. Stuart and Crooks stayed in the fur trade longer, but most of their association with the trade was in the more settled Michilimackinac region. Hunt is an example of an entrepreneur who had only one exposure to the frontier environment of fur trading in the Far Northwest before traveling to the Far East and eventually back to St. Louis, where he remained as a merchant until his death. Although McKenzie remained in the fur trade in the Far Northwest for twenty-five years, which suggests a contradiction to this pattern, two factors should be scrutinized to determine fundamental change or the lack of it in McKenzie's case. First, he was with the Pacific Fur Company for only a few years. Before and after his association with that organization he was associated with the British North West Company and consequently was under a different set of circumstances owing to the greater regulation in the British fur trade. Second, though associated with the fur trade for twenty-five years, his actual physical mobility throughout the Northwest suggests little attachment to any one region or, therefore, to the indigenous problems of that region. Consequently he never interacted with given environments long enough to create a setting for fundamental change to occur.

The history of the American fur-trading frontier is the history of fundamental continuity rather than change. Whether one compares the association between trading establishments and national imperial designs, or the structure of trading associations, or entrepreneurial behavior patterns, they all suggest that same dynamic—continuity.

A recognition of this fact is only the beginning of study because the emphasis then must shift to search for the causatives of continuity. The answer might be provided by categorizing the variables present in respective American frontier settings before comparing frontiers for the presence or absence of these variables. If fur trading is compared to the trans-Appalachian agricultural frontier, which did witness fundamental change, several variables are absent in the former which are present in the latter. The cosmopolitan nature of trading associations provided no commitment to the indigenous development of the Far West. Traders visited the region, completed their transactions, and departed—creating no lasting impact except for the depletion of fur-bearing animals. The fur-trading frontier was not a self-sufficient farm or a sedentary community, it was a frontier that spanned the globe from New York to St. Louis to the Far East. This inherent condition caused the trader to look outward from the frontier region into an international arena.

The Mountain Man's constant exposure to isolated conditions suggests initially a contradiction to the notion of continuity. The Mountain Man historically has been stereotyped as a free spirit, out of place within the bounds of civilization, and a romantic hero who, while close to nature, battled the odds for survival in a wilderness ecosystem. In 1963 William Goetzmann set out to destroy these stereotypes and to establish a more viable interpretation of this phenomenon. Goetzmann asserted that, rather than being misfits of civilization or romantic heroes, the Mountain Men "lived for a chance to exchange their dangerous mountain

47

careers for an advantageous start in civilized life. If one examines their lives and their stated aspirations, one discovers that the Mountain Men, for all their apparent eccentricities, were astonishingly similar to the common men of their time—plain republican citizens of the Jacksonian era."[24] Goetzmann's new stereotype of the Mountain Man as "expectant capitalist" was derived from a statistical review of 446 Mountain Men.[25] Goetzmann found that 259 of the surviving 264 Mountain Men went on to other occupations. Therefore, he concluded, "the Mountain Man was hardly the simple-minded primitive that mythology has made him out to be. Indeed it appears that whenever he had the chance, he exchanged the joys of the rendezvous and the wilderness life for the more civilized excitement of 'getting ahead.'"[26]

The Goetzmann interpretation was left unchallenged until 1975, when Harvey Carter and Marcia C. Spencer questioned Goetzmann's findings. Carter and Spencer attempted to restore the "heroic" image of the Mountain Man with their own statistical survey. Carter and Spencer used "involvement in combat" and "distant wayfaring" as their determining variables. Based on their survey of three hundred Mountain Men, Carter and Spencer concluded that "the heroic stereotype is more valid than many people of the present time would be inclined to admit."[27] To restore the "daring delinquent" stereotype Carter and Spencer employed "drunkenness" and "other faults" as variables and came to similar conclusions.[28] Finally to destroy the Goetzmann "expectant capitalist" stereotype, Carter and Spencer employed four variables: success, moderate success, failure, and negative. The term "negative" was used to refer to those who never indicated that they wanted more from the fur trade than a living.[29]

The striking fallacy of the Carter and Spencer attempt to refute Goetzmann's work lies not in their use of statistics but in their choice of variables and in the simple fact that these are *non sequiturs*. In attempting to restore the Mountain Man as a romantic hero, it is difficult to see how geographical range relates to heroics or, in the case of the other variable, how combat is a variable that can be applied only to Mountain Man behavior patterns. Spatially the environmental setting of the fur-trading frontier was the same for all traders. In other words, the environment presented similar problems to all those exposed to it. It is difficult to see from the work completed on the subject so far how the Mountain Men responded to these environmental pressures differently than others who were exposed to it. Spatially seen in an international context and chronologically placed at the end of the commercial revolution, Mountain Men behaved like entrepreneurs from the beginning of the era. They sought opportunity in high-profit, high-risk ventures wherever that may have carried them.

Carter and Spencer employ "drunkenness" and "other faults" as variables to restore the image of the Mountain Man as a creature not able to live within the bounds of civilization. This hardly qualifies as an empirical test. Does drunkenness and other forms of deviant behavior make one any less of an "expectant capitalist?"

A far more valid test of the effects of frontier isolation on the behavior of Mountain Men might be to compare individual behavior before, during, and after their frontier experience. One might expect to find continuity in behavior as the rule rather than the exception.

Finally, to destroy the Goetzmann portrayal of the Mountain Man as "expectant capitalist," Carter and Spencer again use the four variables: success, moderate success, failure and negative. Again the variables present conclusions that do not follow from their premise: the low rate of success by itself means little since it is the intent, not the outcome, that would determine whether or not the Mountain Man was an "expectant capitalist." When the tenets of historical inquiry are applied it appears that the Goetzmann stereotype has withstood the challenge. His "expectant capitalist" interpretation certainly reinforces the idea of continuity in behavior patterns outlined in this chapter.[30]

Mountain Men, like other fur traders, must be viewed in terms of the extrinsic factors that affected their lives. An environment compatible with the existing tenets of mercantile capitalism, the temporary exposure to frontier conditions, and the international arena of the fur trade all served to diminish the insulation of the fur-trading frontier and, therefore, the possibilities for fundamental change.

CHAPTER 3

The Ranching Frontier:
From Mercantile Capitalism
to Industrial Capitalism

The trans-Mississippi ranching frontier also experienced little or no fundamental change as a result of intrinsic factors. Much like the fur-trading frontier, its history is essentially that of continuity rather than innovation. The lack of fundamental change on the ranching frontier, as on the fur-trading frontier, is clear when one compares its business practices to those already established at the inception of the frontier. The cattlemens' prefrontier behavior patterns and those actually exhibited on the frontier reveal continuity.

If continuity and not fundamental change is characteristic of the ranching frontier, an explanation is needed. It lies in the relationship between the number of interacting links, the degree of insulation, and the degree of indigenous development. The interacting links present in the ranching frontier were numerous enough to prevent the insulation and consequently the indigenous development necessary for fundamental change.

The western scholar usually associates the ranching frontier with the vast trans-Mississippi West, post-Civil War cattle industry. In terms of cattle's national impact, this perspective is correct. It nevertheless lacks the necessary perspective for comparatively viewing cattle in the context of other historical developments previous to and contemporary to ranching.

Historians of American ranching usually attribute its antecedents either to the Spanish or colonial American cattle industry. This perspective has merit, since cattle were not indigenous to the western hemisphere. Old World joint-stock companies exported them to the American colonies until the middle of the seventeenth century, when domestic production of beef was adequate for the colonists' needs.[1]

Initially the cattle industry was an adjunct to general colonial agricultural practices. A specialized cattle industry first appeared in the Piedmont regions of the southern colonies, a region deemed unsuitable for farming. The Piedmont cattle industry, although never as large as that of the Great Plains, did manage to accumulate individual herds as large as six thousand head. The methods of production, however, were similar. Colonial ranchers combined open grazing with "stock-penning," where cattle were driven to enclosed areas for branding and identification. Cattle destined for market were driven along trails, much like Plains cattle, to marketing terminals in Baltimore, Philadelphia, and other large eastern cities.[2] Lewis Gray, the noted southern agricultural historian, has mentioned the similarities between colonial cattle ranching and Great Plains ranching: "Undoubtedly the herding industry in the English Colonies bore a close resemblance to the industry in Texas and in other Spanish Colonies, a similarity which is probably attributable to the fact that similar circumstances led to similar adaptations."[3]

Some would even suggest that the communities which arose around the penning areas resembled the famous Kansas cow towns. "Abilene and Dodge City in the boom trail-driving days had nothing on one of these cowpen communities. Horse thieves and cattle rustlers mingled with honest yokels. The tin dipper of the moonshiner was never idle. Wrestling matches and foot races were the healthiest of the boisterous activities of the camp."[4] By the early nineteenth century, the lure of new pasturing regions coupled with pressures immigrating farmers exerted in the older regions caused the ranching industry to move to the Ohio Valley. Here, four major grassland areas developed in western Kentucky, east-central Ohio, northwest Indiana and central and southern Illinois.

In the Ohio Valley a new factor was introduced to the cattle production process. As the cattle industry spread over the Middle West, earlier grazing regions, beginning with those in Ohio, began to serve as fattening centers for the newer grazing regions of Indiana and Illinois. In the early nineteenth century only about one-half of the cattle in Ohio were native to the territory, the rest having been brought in as stockers for fattening. As the fattening centers developed so too did a specialized corn industry, thus creating an economic symbiosis between stocker cattle areas, feedlot operations, and the corn industry. By 1834 this relationship had fully matured in Ohio and was spreading westward. By 1850 the corn belt had reached Indiana and, by the end of the Civil War, had spread to Illinois and Iowa, while the Plains cattle industry was beginning to develop in Texas.[5]

The Plains cattle industry also owes its origins to the Spanish who brought cattle with them in the course of their eighteenth-century exploration of the American Southwest. While serious efforts to raise cattle are usually attributed to the period of colonization that began with Juan de Onate in 1598, the development of the industry is usually attributed to the Spanish missionaries.[6] Those who argue for the Spanish origins of the American cattle industry point to the continuity of such institutions and practices as the roundup and branding techniques and to such implements as the Spanish saddle and the lariat.

The debate surrounding the origins of American ranching is perhaps too provincial. American ranching developed in the context of the practices of the commercial revolution—whether they were Spanish, Dutch, French, or British in origin. Ranching is best studied in terms of its inherent environmental demands and of how individuals, regardless of nationality, responded to those demands. As a commodity of exchange, cattle needed to be prepared for market (fattened); separated from unfit specimens (cut out); identified (branded); and finally delivered to the consumer (driven by trail). Piedmont cattlemen, Spanish cattlemen, and later American cattlemen all met these basic requirements. Unfortunately, superficial differences have dominated the debate over American ranching origins, detracting from the more fundamental similarities that actually existed.

Viewed within the context of the commercial revolution, cattle, along with spice and furs, represented just another example of a high-profit-potential-high-risk venture. A fortune awaited anyone who could successfully solve the marketing problems associated with early ranching. Distance, bad weather, Indian raids, disease, and dissident farmers were all western manifestations of marketing obstacles that had plagued mercantile capitalists since the beginning of the Age of Discovery.

Early Texas cattlemen, like their Spanish predecessors, were interested in cattle mainly for hides and tallow. Increasingly, however, cattle were driven to regional market outlets, the largest being New Orleans, and sold for food consumption. In order for the cattle industry to realize its full profit potential, however, the cattle needed to be delivered to the developing urban centers of the Northeast and Midwest. A few enterprising venturers, beginning with Edward Piper in 1846, actually drove herds of cattle across country to the Ohio Valley where they were fattened and slaughtered. In 1853 an Illinois merchant drove a small herd from Texas directly to New York City. The drive consumed almost a year and a half. The time, risk, and number of cattle that could be feasibly delivered to the East made this procedure untenable.[7]

While these entrepreneurs attempted to take the product to market in its natural state, others tried to develop a nonperishable beef product. Gail Borden was one of these individuals. He attempted to boil the beef down to a pasty consistency having only ten percent of its original weight. The substance then was mixed with

55

flour to produce a meat biscuit. Borden drew considerable attention to his venture; unfortunately, army contracts he depended on to keep his business solvent in its initial years never were forthcoming, and the venture failed.[8] Richard King was another individual who attempted to produce a nonperishable beef product. He injected salt brine into the veins of butchered cattle as a preservative. The notion of embalmed beef was so distasteful, however, that this venture also was short-lived.[9] The true potential of the Plains cattle industry would not be realized until conditions were right, at the end of the Civil War, for its marketing problems to be solved.

At the war's end, railroad construction began with renewed vigor. The conflict also had an impact on the supply of cattle in Texas. While the nation was at war, Texas cattle were left untended to multiply, thus creating an enormous surplus eagerly sought after for northern markets. The surplus in turn depressed the price of cattle to a point where they could be purchased for three to five dollars a head and sold in the North for ten times that amount. When early Texas entrepreneurs saw tremendous potential in cattle, their entrepreneurial instincts were correct. Following the Civil War, they would begin to realize that potential.

Beginning in 1865 thousands of cattle made the spring trek to Sedalia, Missouri, the first rail terminal for early southern Plains ranchers. Although the extension of the railroad to south-central Missouri significantly shortened the cattle drive, conditions were still not ideal for efficient cattle marketing. The Sedalia trail crossed

56

Indian territory where cattlemen were forced to pay toll charges. In addition to such factors as bad weather, stampedes, and disease, the last leg of the trail covered territory that farmers were rapidly settling. Missouri farmers, fearful of the tick fever many Texas cattle carried, increasingly banded together to prevent Texas ranchers from entering the state.

While early Texas ranchers sought to solve their marketing problems, an Illinois stockman, Joseph McCoy, was busy trying to solve the same problems at the receiving end of the marketing process. In 1867 McCoy set out to locate a site in Kansas that could serve as an ideal railroad terminal point. After several railroads and several Kansas communities rejected his scheme, McCoy convinced the citizens of Abilene, Kansas, and officials of the Hannibal and St. Joseph Railroad that his idea had great potential. After an initial period of instability McCoy's venture rose to monumental proportions. In 1870 alone over 300,000 cattle were driven to Abilene. As these cattle drives proved successful, railroads expanded to other communities, giving birth to such famous Kansas cattle towns as Ellsworth, Newton, Wichita, and, perhaps the most famous of all, Dodge City.[10]

The early Plains cattle industry's development was neither insular nor indigenous. The increased market for cattle was not created within the confines of the ranching frontier environment. Nor was the rapid multiplication of cattle during the war years an indigenously produced phenomenon. In both cases outside factors caused developments within the frontier.

In addition to the continuity of business practices and the extrinsic factors affecting the development of ranching, there was a continuity in entrepreneurial behavior patterns that most early Texas cattlemen shared. It seems as minimal as on the fur-trading frontier. Ranchers, unlike fur traders, were exposed to frontier conditions for great lengths of time; however, like the fur trader, ranchers were linked to the nation in a number of significant ways. In another comparison, the temporal parameters of the ranching frontier insured that technology would provide a lower degree of insulation than the trans-Appalachian pioneer farmer experienced, who also was exposed to frontier conditions for longer periods of time.

This continuity rose from the ranching environment, which did not call for behavior that was different from the behavior exhibited by cattlemen in their precattle frontier experiences. Sketches of Richard King, George Littlefield, Charles Goodnight, John Iliff, and Nelson Story illustrate this point. Their careers are well known, and material on them is readily available. These men, however, are usually viewed as great men in conscious control of their destinies. Free of compelling forces, their strong and intelligent free will determined success. Western scholarship would be better served if studies about cattlemen, about all frontier dwellers, concentrated on preconceived world views that, in different environments, may or may not have changed. Frontiersmen should be viewed as problem solvers acting within a limited range of options that circumstances of their own internal makeup and external surroundings placed before them.

58

As problem solvers, early cattlemen shared a pattern of behavior that saw them repeatedly reinvesting profits as they moved from venture to venture. They did not specialize in any one commodity, and the nature of the ventures varied greatly until significant returns were realized.

Richard King, for example, was a violin maker's apprentice in New York City before he fled to the sea as a cabin boy. He ended up in South Texas in 1846 with little capital to his name. He then took a position as a river boat pilot on the Rio Grande River, a major windfall at this particular time because the Mexican War provided plenty of opportunity for an enterprising individual to deliver supplies to the battlefields in Mexico. In four years King and his partner, Mifflin Kennedy, owned a fleet of river boats and were making a good profit for their efforts. From his base of operation in Brownsville, King could speculate on the great potential the area possessed for raising cattle when a market was available. King took some of the surplus capital from his river boat operation and invested it in 75,000 acres of land along the Nueces River. This would become the core of the famous King ranching empire. By 1860 King, although he never realized the ultimate potential of his ranching enterprise, foresaw such a bright future that he expanded his operation. In classic mercantile-capitalist fashion King took on a partner to obtain the capital needed for expansion. The Civil War meanwhile only increased an already profitable river boat operation and provided the necessary capital for additional expansion. By 1865 King's original 75,000 acres had grown to 300,000 acres. King and Kennedy in 1868 were sufficiently confident of the future that they dissolved their partnership and pursued their fortunes individually. The best was yet to come as the King ranch, like others, profited during the cattle boom years of the 1870s and early 1880s. When King died in 1885 his ranching operation included half a million acres.[11]

This story typifies the careers of entrepreneurs who used the profits from one venture to launch another and more profitable venture. Had cattle not been so lucrative, King could have used his surplus capital for investment in another venture, unrelated to cattle.

George Littlefield's entry into the cattle business followed a similar pattern. Unlike King, Littlefield came to Texas with a large capital base; his family were established cotton farmers in Mississippi. The southern cotton farmer's economic trials and tribulations during the Reconstruction era did not affect Littlefield because he was already making the transition from cotton to cattle. Through various partnership agreements with family members he gradually accumulated significant amounts of land, cattle, and horses. Some cattle came to him in trade through a mercantile firm in which he owned a partnership. When the cattle boom began in the 1870s he was in a position to take full advantage of it. His small mercantile firm and partnership agreements provided the windfall capital necessary for later investment in a larger more profitable venture, the Kansas cattle trade. The profits from his 1870s Kansas trade, in turn, provided the base for the expansion of his original ranching enterprise in the Texas Panhandle. The structure of Littlefield's financial operations in the

1880s was a maze of ranching partnership arrangements scattered all over the West Texas landscape. Littlefield meanwhile personally oversaw his operations from a central office in Austin.[12]

Further to the north, in these early years, much the same entrepreneurial pattern unfolded in the career of John Iliff. He migrated to Kansas from Ohio where his father was a farmer and stock raiser. Iliff rejected an offer of a farm adjacent to his father's, preferring a small stake of five hundred dollars with which to move west. College-educated, he migrated to Kansas and operated a store for three years. This venture provided enough capital to take advantage of the Colorado mining boom. The sale of his store in Kansas provided funds to purchase and transport provisions for another mercantile establishment in Denver. Iliff's Denver store, in turn, provided the capital base to launch yet another adventure, cattle. Like Littlefield, Iliff gradually accumulated cattle in trade for goods in his store. After a year and a half he used some of his capital to invest in a small herd of cattle in Wyoming. The timing and location of Iliff's initial cattle investment was no accident. His entrepreneurial sense perceived the windfall potential of his Wyoming investment, because the construction of the Union Pacific Railroad meant government contracts to food suppliers. From this base, the cattle boom of the 1870s and 1880s allowed him to build one of the largest herds in Colorado and Wyoming—consisting at its peak of almost 50,000 head of cattle. Like King and Littlefield, he gradually expanded his capital base with shrewd speculative ventures and was poised to take full advantage of the cattle boom. Like King and Littlefield, his pattern of behavior suggests that had not cattle become such a lucrative venture, he would have invested elsewhere.[13]

When Iliff supplied beef to the railroad workers he did not have enough cattle to realize this market's potential. He therefore obtained additional cattle from Charles Goodnight, another early cattle entrepreneur whose career exhibited the same patterns as those of King, Littlefield, and Iliff. Goodnight, like King and Iliff, had little capital with which to begin. A keen entrepreneurial sense, coupled with windfall opportunities, served as the base for his later fortune. Goodnight, for example, looked for opportunity to New Mexico, where government contracts awaited those who could supply military personnel and reservation Indians with beef. Forming a partnership with Oliver Loving, Goodnight gathered a herd in 1866 for a drive to Fort Sumner. Cattle not sold at this military installation were driven further north to Denver where Loving sold them to Iliff for his Wyoming venture. Meanwhile Goodnight took the surplus capital from the Fort Sumner sale back to Texas to purchase more cattle. Again the pattern is similar. The returns from the original venture provided the capital for future cattle drives. After Loving was killed along the trail back from Denver, Goodnight continued the business connection with Iliff. Goodnight prospered through his northern connection until the Panic of 1873 ruined him, along with many other cattle speculators. Economic misfortune did not deter Goodnight's vision of the bright future in store for cattlemen. After several years Goodnight set out to establish a ranch in the Texas Panhandle. Goodnight possessed the skill to succeed in the cattle business; however, capital was the missing link that could launch such an enterprise on the grand scale necessary to realize its potential. John Adair, a wealthy Irishman, had the necessary capital to invest in Goodnight's venture. This was the beginning of what would become the famous million-acre JA ranch. The Goodnight-Adair ranching venture netted the partners over $500,000 in five years. Later Goodnight withdrew from the partnership to purchase his own ranching operation.[14]

Finally there is Nelson Story, who is credited with beginning the ranching industry in the Northwest. The pattern of Story's career and his entry into the cattle business is similar to those already outlined. He migrated from Ohio to Kansas where he cut wood and sold fence posts for a living. Story's first windfall came from condemned government wagons that he had an opportunity to purchase at greatly reduced prices. The wagons were used in a freighting venture that carried him to the Colorado gold fields where he became interested in prospecting but experienced little success. He followed the gold rush to Montana where his luck changed with a moderate strike that netted him $30,000. This windfall launched another venture, this time in cattle. Story traveled to Texas and purchased a thousand head of cattle that he intended to trail north to the Montana gold fields for a quick profit. Story's arrival in Virginia City in 1866 marked the end of a successful journey and the beginning of a fortune. Through shrewd movements from venture to venture, each time increasing his capital base, Story was able to amass a ranching fortune.[15]

The lives of these men illustrate a common pattern of behavior on the part of early cattlemen. Western history would benefit immeasurably if this theme were pursued in greater depth. To date only Lewis Atherton in *The Cattle Kings* has developed this theme at any length. He perceptively concludes that "If anyone explains or offers a universal key to how so many men started without inherited money and became cattle kings, that word would be 'trader.'"[16] Atherton convincingly outlines a typical pattern by which entrepreneurs, although known for their success in ranching, actually acquired the necessary capital base for this enterprise through a series of prior trading ventures unrelated to cattle.

An explanation for the continuity may lie in the number of significant interacting links present on the ranching frontier and the compatibility of its environment to previous experiences. Early cattlemen exhibited a uniform mercantile-capitalist mentality interested in trading and swapping anything deemed profitable. Their names have been associated with the cattle industry only because it was the venture that brought them fame and fortune. The early cattlemen's entrepreneurial behavior patterns constituted an embedded, opportunity-oriented frame of mind that would remain intact unless traumatic changes in the environment were to jolt it. The ranching environment did not do this; it only reinforced entrepreneurial patterns. The mercantile capitalist, therefore, had only a tenuous association with his physical location. It was a business outpost, and not the setting for his social and political and cultural experience.

Cattle, as the commodity of trade, were also an interacting link. In order to produce a profitable return, however, cattle had to be traded or sold to another individual, most likely in another section of the country. The necessity of this transaction effectively created an economic symbiosis between the cattlemen and the receivers of his product. The symbiosis, in turn, cast local affairs, whether economic, political, or cultural, in a broader perspective, thus preventing true indigenous development and consequently fundamental change.

The history of the early ranching frontier is essentially a history of continuity in the business practices inherited from the Spanish as well as the colonial and Ohio Valley cattlemen. It is difficult to see how the frontier experience fundamentally altered previous behavior patterns. These trends need to be coupled with the cattlemen's cultural and intellectual makeup in a new and more complex study of ranching history.

As the Plains cattle industry experienced its years of phenomenal growth in the 1870s and 1880s, the frontier environment changed. This change called for different responses from those already engaged in it and brought different kinds of individuals to the ranges. While an opportunity-oriented frame of mind characterized the early ranching frontier, the later ranching era was clearly more industry-minded. Specifically, later cattlemen concentrated more on developing one industry than on casting about for new ventures to invest in. Despite this shift in orientation the net impact was similar. Institutions and individuals of the later ranching era also did not change measurably from their pre-cattle frontier experiences.

As the cattle industry spread northward to the Texas Panhandle, Colorado, Wyoming, Montana, and the Dakotas, new circumstances altered it. The high price of beef and such promotional books as James Brisbin's *The Beef Bonanza or How to get Rich on the Plains . . .* attracted new investors from both America and Europe.[17] Brisbin's book outlined what was to become the stereotypical image of the Plains cattle industry. It suggested that cattle cared for and naturally reproduced themselves, thus increasing the owner's worth with little expenditure. Brisbin's book was especially widely read in Europe and is partly credited for the large influx of European money into the western ranges. The influx of new investors affected the economic ecology that had developed between land, man, and animal. The resultant overpopulation of cattle not only depressed the price of beef but also depleted grazing lands. These factors—when combined with the reality of the increased cost of raising cattle as a result of such factors as winter feeding and the higher cost of labor— produced at best an unstable economic situation. The cattle surplus drove down the price of each unit so much that the industry could not withstand the devastating droughts and harsh winters of 1884 and 1885 without a total collapse of its structure. The usual historical interpretation suggests that these factors, when combined with the impact of fencing and the increased competition farmers and sheepmen exerted for land, account for the demise of the cattle boom on the Plains.[18]

There is nothing incorrect about the stated causatives for the decline of the ranching frontier. However, when placed in the context of the cosmopolitan model I propose, it seems to lack the dimension which suggests that the number of interacting links present were significant enough to tie it closely to the economic factors affecting the rest of the nation. More and more ranchers were becoming acutely aware that cattle were no longer a short-term, high-return investment opportunity. Cattlemen, like their eastern business counterparts, were caught up in national economic trends and patterns that would cause both groups to strive for stability through efficient management.

A comparative view of later ranching practices with those of eastern business would profit Western historians immensely.[19] The parallels are striking and should be pursued further. Alfred D. Chandler succinctly outlined the process involved in the development of large business units during the late nineteenth century.[20] Central to this process was the rise of a large urban market and the consequent innovations in organization and marketing techniques for taking advantage of this opportunity. National marketing organizations and the consolidation of production factors "under a single manufacturing department" were the principle changes in business structure. Consolidation and integration therefore were simple business responses to obstacles in the new industrial business environment. Obstacles such as the combination of low production and high unit costs could at once impede efficiency. The rise of big business in Chandler's view resulted in "large-scale buying, more rational routing of raw material and finished products, more systematic plant lay-out, and plant location in relation to materials."[21]

The thrust of Chandler's argument is that "costs, rather than interfirm competition, began to determine prices."[22] Placed in the context of the later ranching period, might not the increased emphasis on sound management techniques represent a different manifestation of the same trend? By the same token, might not the increased use of fencing be partially viewed as a cost-cutting device because it diminished the number of labor units needed and made more efficient use of available pasture lands? Finally, might not the consolidation of large ranching units be viewed from this perspective?

Chandler also states that eastern businesses attempted to stabilize prices not only through integrating marketing procedures but also through the creation of interfirm organizations. Trade associations were formed in all of the major industries to eliminate harmful competition and to promote the general welfare of the member firms. Were cattlemen's associations the rancher's response to the same external factors that stimulated growth of trade associations in the East? Cattlemen's associations mediated disputes, kept brand books, and organized *de facto* law enforcement units—all as responses to factors that tended to produce instability or generally affect the welfare of the ranching industry. Perhaps the histories of such great cattlemen's associations as the Wyoming Stock Grower's Association, The Colorado Stock Growers' Association, and others should be rewritten with this perspective in mind.[23]

Control and consolidation for greater efficiency were very much a part of the later ranching era. Perhaps the histories of such ranching empires as the XIT and the JA and of such organizations as the Matador Land and Cattle Company and the Swan Land and Cattle Company should be rewritten to take into account the forces and responses associated with eastern industrial consolidation and growth.[24] This perspective would add dimension to existing studies that suggest that large profits brought big investors, which meant consolidation at the expense of small ranches. The underlying impulse of this interpretation leaves human greed as the only causative factor. This premise is much the same as the one that until recently influenced studies of industrial growth during the Gilded Age. Recently, however, scholars have shown this period to be more dimensional by revealing a business logic in the growth process. Ironically, histories of industrial growth in the East may be more useful to the western scholar of ranching than existing topical works on the subject.[25]

Western historians also must ask what impact the later ranching environment had on individuals who came to it. A study should be undertaken to compare the careers of the cattlemen who did not begin ranching until the boom years of the 1870s and early 1880s and those whose careers date back to the pre-Civil War

69

era. Did the fraternity of later ranchers comprise the cosmopolitan mixture characteristic of the early Texas cattlemen? Did later ranchers share an entrepreneurial behavior pattern such as I have suggested for the early ranchers? If they did, what is the nature of the pattern and what might be the causatives for its existence?

An initial view of the later ranchers suggests that although the structure of their industry was similar they were otherwise an extremely diverse lot, not even sharing the entrepreneurial behavior pattern attributed to the earlier cattlemen. The characters ranged from Dan Casement, a Princeton graduate who used his father's Colorado ranch to conduct experiments in Social Darwinism, to Gregor Lang, an Irish ideologue who came to the western ranges to realize his passion for democracy.[26] The later ranching period also contained characters like C. M. Oelrich, who could be seen riding up to the famed Cheyenne Club in a coach-and-four decked out with properly attired coachmen; and Conrad Kohrs, the middle-class German butcher turned cattleman, who with his wife traveled all over the world to meet with high society at such events as the Chicago World's Fair and the Mardi Gras and the opera season in New York City.[27] Western historians must find a context for this behavior or suffer the criticism that their discipline is provincial and episodic with little to offer the serious scholar. This behavior may be better understood if it is viewed in the same context as historians of the Gilded Age view the life styles of the industrial nouveau riche in the East. Ostentatious behavior was characteristic of both life styles.[28]

CHAPTER 4

The Mining Frontier: Continuity
in the Far West

Much like the ranching and fur-trading frontier, the mining frontier and its scenario of events and cast of characters has been neatly stereotyped. The mere mention of western mining trips into consciousness an image of the bearded prospector smitten with gold fever and of his trusty mule heavily laden with supplies. The prospector carried out his wanderlust in a setting replete with bustling tent cities, boom towns, gambling dens, dance halls, and prostitutes. Episodic accounts depicting these stereotypical ingredients are in no short supply.

On a scholarly level, mining frontier history has been closely associated with the Turner thesis and its contentions concerning the furtherance of democratic political procedures and social equality.[1] Indeed it is difficult to turn one's back on these themes: they are ever present in the mining frontier. Even before Turner a noted mining scholar, Charles Shinn, pointed to the same developments: "The mines put all men for once upon a level. Clothes, money, manners, family connections, letters of introduction, never before counted so little. . . . Social and financial inequalities between man and man were together swept out of sight."[2] Shinn saw these traits as the fruition of this country's Teutonic heritage. His study first appeared in 1884 and it was only a matter of one decade before the same characteristics became central to Turner's hypothesis. Turner, however, unlike Shinn, rejected Teutonic ancestry as the causative factor and instead found it to be the indigenous effect of the frontier environment. Nevertheless, whether Teutonic or frontier in origin, such factors as mining codes, vigilance committees, and *de facto* courts seem to verify the notion that the American West did indeed spawn or at least amplify democratic political and social development as Turner had suggested.[3]

Most western historians would tend to support this notion. A noted mining scholar, Duane Smith, states the proposition directly: "democracy, under the leveling influence of poverty and a fresh start in a strange land reached a zenith."[4] A casual reading of this statement might suggest that Turner might indeed have a valid application to the mining frontier. In fact, they only represent an endorsement of the fact that institutions had to be created where there were none before. In order for the Turner thesis to be truly applicable, democratic assumptions must have been born on the mining frontier or have evolved as a radical departure from previous practices and assumptions. Few historians would suggest that the conceptual foundations of American history by 1848 were not quite democratic. The mining frontier was not the originator in a Turnerian sense but a setting that reinforced existing notions. Ironically, therefore, a better perspective of political and social behavior on the mining frontier can be gained if that behavior is seen in terms of national trends that occurred in the decades prior to the initial rush in California.

It is not enough, however, to contend that the mining frontier is solely the history of continuity. The renowned mining scholar Rodman Paul suggests that the mining frontier was "a curious blending of the new and the familiar, of innovation and imitation."[5] Using the categories of fundamental and superficial change suggested in this text, western scholars can make further distinctions.[6] Mining laws serve as a good illustration of how these distinctions can be applied. On the question of borrowed, versus innovative, mining laws, Thomas Rickard, a respected early historian of western mining, stated that

The right to locate a mining claim, and to hold it against all comers, until abandoned, was generally admitted. This basic idea of mining law had been brought by the adventurers to California from other lands; it was the traditional right of the miner, as much in the seven mine-cities of Harz as in the stannaries of Devonshire and Cornwall.[7]

Although in general most scholars concur with Rickard, some more refined exceptions have been pointed out. For example Rodman Paul states that while western mining codes followed English and Spanish precedent, local adaptations on the rules of ownership of veins did take place. Californians excluded surface boundaries of claims in place of the right of the individual to follow a vein wherever it might lead him. This and other originations in mining law tend to confuse the patterns of continuity otherwise suggested, unless the superficial and fundamental change categories are applied. Are those aspects of mining law considered unique to western mining, fundamental changes from previous patterns, or merely superficial manifestations of change? For example, the principle that the original locator of a claim had the right to it as long as he worked it was universal in scope. This is fundamental to all placer stage mining law. Qualifications of this fundamental principle—such as the size of the claim or the definition of boundaries—were varied and represented only superficial change.

American mining scholarship should also broaden its time-place perspective to view mining as a universal phenomenon, and concentrate on the historical process at work on mining frontiers regardless of time and place. A comparison between the Georgia gold rush in the early 1830s and the trans-Mississippi West gold rush several decades later can simply illustrate this point. More specifically one can list characteristics commonly recognized as part of the trans-Mississippi mining frontier scene and then suggest that each of the characteristics was also a part of the Georgia gold rush scene. Stories of chance discoveries were common. There was a rapid influx of diverse groups of people. A process of social leveling took place. Prices were high and credit almost nonexistent. The itinerancy rate was very high. Mining communities boasted "dens of iniquity," images which stood in contrast to concerted efforts of many people to insure stable community development. There were also bizarre and unusual characters, easily transformed into legend. When the miners, merchants, and professional people moved on to new strikes, the deserted communities either became ghost towns or changed the premise of their existence. At the end of the placer stage of mining, outside capital took over and directed the next stages of mining development. The trail led to North Georgia where, beginning in 1814, prospectors began to invade mineral areas the Cherokees then inhabited. The main rush, however, did not ensue until 1828, when a hunter accidentally kicked over a rock to discover gold beneath it. Although this is the incident that most point to as setting off the rush, there are other tales of chance discoveries. There is the story of the slave who presented his master with a peculiar-looking rock he found in the woods that had gold ore imbedded in it.[8]

Once the news of gold spread, the North Georgia region was flooded with eager gold seekers. Since the ore was on Cherokee land, federal troops were sent in to keep the miners out. These efforts were to no avail. Succumbing to the pressures brought on by the sudden influx of people, the state of Georgia created a county out of the region, bringing it under white jurisdiction. This marks the beginning of the unimpeded gold rush.[9]

Mining activities in Georgia became centered in two communities, Dahlonega and Auraria. As in the far western mining communities, growth was sudden and dramatic. In 1832, a year after its founding, Auraria had between twelve and fifteen law offices, twenty stores, and five taverns. The number of law offices might indicate, as it did in the Far West, that settling claims disputes made the mining frontier a lawyer's paradise. At its peak, Auraria had 1,000 permanent residents and 10,000 itinerants, but it faded with the boom. In 1854 Auraria had only five merchants left and became a ghost town.[10] Dahlonega's population rose from 800 to 5,000.

As in the case of Auraria and numerous far western mining communities, merchants, lawyers, bankers, barbers, doctors, and artisans of all types moved to Dahlonega to make money off of the miners. As news of the California gold strike reached Georgia, however, Dahlonega's population dramatically shrank to just a few hundred people. This amazing transference took less than a week. But unlike Auraria, Dahlonega did not become a ghost town; earlier it had been made the county seat and hence assumed some local importance.[11] This boom-bust pattern is familiar to most western mining scholars.

Inflation was another characteristic that the Georgia gold rush shared with the far western gold rush. In 1834, in Auraria, corn sold for 75¢ to 87 1/2¢ per bushel. Flour sold for $10.00 a barrel and butter commanded 25¢ a pound.[12] In Virginia at the same time a barrel of flour cost $4.81. Two years earlier, in the New York City market, flour cost $6.00 a barrel. These figures indicate merit in calling for a more thorough study of questions concerning capital, credit, and inflationary patterns in the Georgia gold regions.[13]

Much as in the far western mining communities, newspapers played an important role in creating the outside world's image of the Georgia gold rush, as well as in stimulating more immigration. In addition to regional newspapers sending special correspondents to the area, the mining communities spawned seven newspapers of their own.[14] Through these newspapers, a stereotypical boom town image was created. The outside world learned that all manner of vice and crime was rampant in the gold region. Gambling, drinking, and fraternizing with prostitutes were the order of the day.

As in the Far West, many colorful tales of bizarre characters emanated from the gold fields. The noted southern novelist William Gilmore Simms created the legendary Guy Rivers. Guy Rivers supposedly inhabited a cave ten miles from Auraria and spent most of his waking hours terrorizing the community. Although Rivers was fictitious, his legend grew until it became indistinguishable from reality.[15] Later tours of the region included a stop at the cave Rivers supposedly inhabited. Simms certainly was imbued with the spirit of the phenomenon when he wrote: "It is a tale of Georgia—a tale of the miners—of a frontier and wild people, and the events are precisely such as may occur among a people & in a region of that character."[16]

Thus the image of the Georgia gold rush was created much in the same way as in the Far West. To be sure, these communities were not stable. Boom town environments, whether for gold, oil, or tourist trade, produced a high rate of itinerancy and with it much irresponsible behavior that was not in the interest of the permanent population.

Within the communities the pressure of population fostered a concerted effort to deal with crime and sanitation problems. In Georgia, committees devised plans to insure stability within the community.[17]

Like the far western mining frontier, the Georgia gold scene was viewed as an arena where class lines were obliterated. Contemporary observers of the Georgia gold rush suggested that even the slaves employed in the mines were treated like white hired labor. This equalizing tendency as well as the "dens of iniquity" are captured nicely in a poem inspired by Auraria.

> Wend you to the Cherokee?
>   Where the Indian girls are prattling;
> Where everyone is conscience free,
>   And "chuck-luck" boxes loud are rattling;
> Where gin by the barrel full is drank, —
>   And whites and blacks are all the same;
> Where no respect is paid to rank,
>   But every ones of equal fame.[18]

The poem, of course, is a sarcastic response to allegedly dangerous democratic tendencies occurring in Auraria. In fact part of the fear of crime stemmed from the influx of slaves who were used in the mines.

The economic trends and demographic patterns of the Georgia gold rush were also quite similar to those of the Far West. News of new strikes caused a sudden and feverish migration from one location to another. Once the surface placer deposits disappeared, prospectors, not having the capital to continue to mine the remaining deposits, simply moved on to places where gold could be mined with little capital. Not only does one find considerable movement within the Georgia gold fields but, with the California strike in 1848, many Georgians took their experience and ambitions west to seek fortunes. One can picture the Dahlonega assayer pleading with miners not to leave for California when he said, "Why go to California? There's gold in them thar hills. In that ridge lies more gold than man ever dreamed of. There's millions in it."[19] The miners did leave, however, and with their departure the frontier stage ended — paving the way for the next stage of mining in Georgia.

By the 1870s, northern- and European-capitalized corporations did most of the mining in Georgia. As in the Far West, hydraulic and deep rock mining required a great deal of capital and the corporate structure was the logical response. By the dawn of the twentieth century, the Dahlonega Mining Company and the British-Georgia Gold Mining Company were the largest gold mining operations in the East.[20] Historians might profit from a comparative investigation of outside investment in the Georgia gold fields and the more studied investment patterns in the far western mines.[21]

This cursory comparison between Georgia mining and far western mining illustrates that western mining history may be too involved with its own sense of uniqueness. Historians must be concerned as much with universal historical processes as with occurrences of specific places and times.

In the chapters on fur trading and ranching, prosopographic reviews suggested a behavioral continuity between prefrontier and frontier experiences. These sketches concentrated only on entrepreneurial behavior patterns to demonstrate a cast of mind oriented by mercantile-capitalistic concerns for opportunity. The mining frontier can be studied by employing the same techniques with some qualifications. On the fur-trading and ranching frontiers, the initial migration was quite selective, partly owing to the economic nature of these frontiers. Large profits could not be anticipated without a considerable capital investment that was usually beyond the capacity of single individuals. In addition considerable skill was required to manage all of the economic variables concerned with acquiring and disposing of the desired raw product.

Migration to the mining frontier, however, was not so selective. No doubt it attracted a more diverse group of people than any other frontier. Despite the diversity, the attracting force was the same—economic betterment with little expenditure. The entrepreneurial skills on the mining frontier were not so demanding as on other frontiers. Unlike fur traders and cattlemen, miners did not have to worry about the timing involved in securing and disposing of the raw product. Theirs was merely a question of finding it.

A reexamination of the mining prospector is needed. Most studies have concentrated on the exploits of individual miners with little attention to the phenomenon of miners as a group. The prospector image has been locked in, much like the Mountain Man was until William Goetzmann gave the latter group some logical behavioral pattern. At present the prospectors' behavior is explained only in vague terms, such as having succumbed to "wanderlust" or to the compulsive drive to find the big strike. Such characteristics existed among prospectors and have been chronicled in episodic descriptions of countless bizarre figures, but did the directionless, wandering prospector actually represent the majority who came to the mining fields? An examination of miners' diaries and journals in fact may reveal just the opposite pattern—both for those who struck it rich and for those who realized only small or modest returns. A random view of some of these prospectors should illustrate this point.

John Eagle went to California from New York in 1852, leaving his wife and children behind to attend to his mercantile business in New York. Eagle's flight to California did not represent the stereotypical wanderlust pattern because he continued to show a strong commitment to his New York community and business. "My absence from you and the children only tends to increase the attachments to 'Home Sweet Home' and causes me to look forward with pleasure to the time when I expect to return to the bosom of my family and friends," he wrote his wife.[22]

Thomas Lewis represents another example of an individual who went to the gold fields without an apparently crazed state of mind. Lewis left Ohio as a foundry worker and after a period in the gold fields returned to that occupation. The extra capital acquired as a result of his mining efforts was used "to keep a toy and confectionary shop for the girls [his daughters] to attend to it."[23]

The stereotypical wanderlust instinct is not found in

the mining career of George Cornell, who went to the gold fields in 1852 from his New York home. Cornell's letters to his wife convey a feeling that he was not counting on making an immediate and enormous fortune but rather hoped to improve the lot of his family in more modest terms. Family debts apparently made these improvements necessary. Reference to loan interest payments and to his wife's occasional stints as a shop laborer seem to bear out this contention. His wife's employment outside the home was a source of irritation to Cornell. He wrote to her, "I think you have enough to do without taking shop work while I am away from home. If I keep well and I can send you all the money you want to live on without taking any work, I hope you will not take any more till I come home."[24] Despite Cornell's contentions that he could send his wife all the money she needed to live on, he was probably speaking of only a modest improvement in life style. "I do want to come home very bad but I will try to stay till I can get something to help ourselves with," he wrote her. "I have ernet $495.75 since I have bin hear have spent $260.89 and lost for work $26.75 have sent home $200.00 so you can see that I have had some money since I have bin here. I would like to have you here and then I could save a great deal more money and live better to."[25]

John Eagle, Thomas Lewis, and George Cornell were individuals who shared the same controlled attitude toward gold mining. From the records it appears that none succumbed to the hysteria usually associated with prospector behavior. Each returned to his home to modestly improve his circumstance either through some small investment or by paying off outstanding debts.

Another kind of prospector who does not fit the wanderlusting stereotype is the one who remained in the gold mining region to pursue other occupations. Charles Pomeroy, a New Yorker by birth, had been involved in a number of enterprises before his migration to California in 1849. Before that he had owned and operated stores and sawmills in Michigan and Indiana. Two years before migrating to the gold fields, he built a blast furnace for manufacturing pig iron in La Porte, Indiana. After four years of mining and farming in California, he was to return to this enterprise. In 1854 he invested in a San Jose foundry business and within a year owned all the shares in the enterprise. In 1866 he sold his foundry business and began a lifelong career as a banker. Gold fever clearly had not struck Pomeroy.[26]

Another representative of this type was George Applegate. Applegate was a very calculating and applied individual before, during, and after his frontier experience. He migrated from a small Missouri community where he had demonstrated early in life a penchant for business affairs. Upon his arrival in California in 1850 he shrewdly saw that money could be made if one were patient, flexible, and willing to work. Shortly after his arrival he concluded that

the old miners are making but little now, and are running all over the country examining the different mines to ascertain where a fortune can be quickest made, and a great many of them I think will never get it, because they will not be contented to work for good wages, but want to find it without much labor, but let me tell you where one makes a fortune in California without working for it 999 go away poorer than they came. . . . Such men are very little account anywhere, and never will be, because any man in California that will use industry can make a much larger amount than he can at home, even at any business he undertakes. A great many will work a few days and then go to the city and spend it. Such work will not do in any country.[27]

While in California Applegate did not wander about looking for the big strike but spent his time buying and selling claims. Applegate admitted making mistakes that resulted in business failures and equated it with gambling. "It is exactly like gambling but a man can make money here all the time trading or mining if he will not be too greedy."[28] Applegate, while maintaining an interest with his father in a considerable claim on the American River, cast about for more stable opportunities. He used his skills as a bookkeeper to enter the employ of several businesses, including a hotel and freight company. This was done instead of moving to Oregon with many other prospectors in the rush of 1852. Applegate's California business affairs were always cast in terms of long-run Missouri business affairs. His letters to his brother talked much of economic matters in Missouri and often contained investment advice to his brother who acted as his agent.

As the rush passed from California to other parts of the West, Applegate began to see great farming potential in California. He tried to convince his family to move to California. He could, he said, "make a fortune here raising hogs and chickens." Furthermore he noted the change in character of California migrants. "Thousands upon thousands of families are coming now from the states, and settling in every part of the country and all of them people of the first class. The *scum* cannot raise the means to bring them here."[29]

In November of 1852 Applegate returned to Missouri to visit his family and attend to business matters associated with his family. He lived in St. Louis with relatives in order to take several college courses in mathematics and accounting before returning to California in 1853. Applegate's economic affairs at this juncture became completely diversified. He was associated with a lumbering enterprise, wheat and hog farming, and he maintained a tavern. Business affairs were a common theme in letters to his brother. The frontier experience did not diminish the importance of such matters in his life.

Finally there is the case of Joseph Aram, who migrated to California for reasons of health. He became engaged in gold mining but soon left the fields for another occupation in the same region. Aram had been a farmer in Ohio, Illinois, and California before the gold strike of 1848. News of the strike prompted him to try his hand at it for several months before returning to the more familiar environs of farming. Aram went on to become a member of the Constitutional Convention of California and later served as a state legislator.[30]

In the case of both Pomeroy and Aram, the mining frontier environment had little impact on previously established behavior patterns. Pomeroy and Aram both remained in California and both returned to their careers in metal manufacturing and farming. Applegate returned to California and displayed the same flexibility that was part of his character in Missouri. Certainly the mining frontier was an exotic place—producing unusual people and circumstances—but the feverish atmosphere perhaps did not affect most miners to the degree that the stereotype suggests. Exotic surroundings did not necessarily stimulate changes in behavior patterns. The mining frontier in some cases, perhaps most, reinforced prefrontier attitudes. For example, William Swain wrote to his brother in 1850 that "Absence from friends has given me a true valuation of them, and also has taught me to appreciate the comforts and blessings of home & above all the circumstances attendant upon the journey combined with reflection have impressed upon my mind a proper appreciation of the overruling hand of an all wise and kind being in the affairs of Mankind."[31]

Or consider the thoughts of another miner, Harvey Lamb, who wrote in 1852: "I think that I can now appreciate the value of a good home and kind and loving friends and if I am ever permitted to reach that home it will require something stronger than 'down town attractions' to aliveate [*sic*] my afections from it."[32]

Thomas Lewis, writing to his wife in 1852, summed up the temptations contained in the mining communities and his rejection of such temptations, and reaffirmed his former life style: "This is a place to try [men's] strength of character and their virtue, every inducement held out to entice them astray, but it is a good place for a hard working family of boys and girls."[33] In another letter Lewis reaffirmed this theme. "My prayer is 'Lead us not into temptation,' &c. If I am blessed with health and strength to get home I shall know how to appreciate the blessings of a home."[34]

Another example of behavioral continuity on the American mining frontier is illustrated in the person of Peter Cool. Cool had strong religious convictions before migrating to the mining frontier. A devout Methodist, Cool spent several years in the chaotic mining environment where alternative life styles seemingly did not affect him. His journal reflected a continued devotion to religious affairs. On one occasion he walked from his community of Amadore to Drytown to purchase a pair of boots because of his "deturmenation to not patronize an[y] on[e] that sells liquor and there was no trading post at Amadore that was *temperate*."[35] When Cool left the gold fields he became an ordained Methodist minister and created a pattern of continuity in his postfrontier life.

When dealing with the careers of individual miners or groups of miners, historians should consider the question of the impact of the frontier on preexisting behavior patterns. Depending on the data available, valuable perspectives can be gained. Historians may also wish to reexamine those prospectors who do fit the stereotypical mold, those who did possess a sense of wanderlust that carried them all over the Far West and, in some cases, to other continents. Historians might gain new perspectives of this category of miner if prefrontier behavior patterns are examined. Were these individuals possessed by wanderlust before coming to the mining frontier? Did the mining frontier only exaggerate these already well-established patterns of behavior. For example, in reading the correspondence of Amos Pittman to his mother one can detect a restless devil-may-care attitude. Pittman went to California in 1852 where he prospected for only a short time before departing for Australia. In 1852 he wrote his mother, "I have made up my mind and before this scribbling reaches you I will be ploughing the Blue Pacific once more crying Westward *Ho Ho*. I am going to try my fortune among the gold mines of John Bulls colonies in the Indian Ocean . . ." He went on to characterize himself as a "rolling stone which gathers no moss." Pittman saw himself as a man with a "roving disposition to see the world and I might as well see it while I am young for the sooner I sow my wild oats the better."[36]

In 1853, from Sydney, Australia, he wrote his mother what amounts to a reaffirmation of his expectations of wealth and his determination to get it. "God only knows when I will return home one thing is certain I will never return until I make something worth returning with, for the world owes me a living and I am going to have it. I have come this far for it and I shall not leave without it."[37]

When the data is available historians might do well to ask whether or not the prospectors' behavior was merely an extension of patterns already established in their prefrontier backgrounds. If institutions and behavior patterns are often merely extensions of established practices, historians are dealing with a cosmopolitan environment that fosters only superficial change. As with the other frontiers we've examined, some explanation is needed for the lack of fundamental change on the mining frontier.

Based on the model applied to fur trading, trans-Appalachian agriculture, and ranching, the mining frontier was the least insular of all the frontiers. This is the case because more interacting links existed between that frontier and more established areas. Interacting links are manifested in a number of characteristics inherent to mining. First, mining was the most specialized of all frontiers and consequently the least self-sufficient. Miners more than any other group of frontiersmen were reliant on others for goods and services. Second, because of the temporary nature of any mining operation, the miner never developed the attachment to place that other frontiersmen did. His long-range interests were not served by the local mining scene but by distant communities. Third, the mining frontier evolved along with technological developments and internal improvements that served to link the nation—thus decreasing insulated political, social, and economic pockets. The high degree of specialization, its temporary nature, and the period during which it unfolded served to decrease the degree of insulation and consequently the degree of indigenous development. The mining frontier was outwardly directed, and therefore its environment offered no great challenge to existing beliefs and practices. Mining codes, vigilantism, and people's courts were merely manifestations of democratic instincts already created in an earlier era.

Epilogue

In 1964, W. N. Davis, Jr. reported the results of a survey that he had conducted on the future of the West in American History. The results came as no surprise to the scholarly community because they only reinforced a commonly held notion that the field would perish unless scholars made "fresh efforts in the form of imaginative, modern analysis of the large issues and of imaginative, modern synthesis of the separate ends."[1]

With some notable exceptions, this cry seems to have fallen upon deaf ears, and those scholars associated with Great Plains settlement seem to have been the most immune to such criticisms. Perhaps this is so because they have had Walter Prescott Webb's classic work *The Great Plains* to fall back on. Webb's stress on the region's uniqueness offered a clear and concise justification for its study. Its uniqueness began with its geological formation and carried through to its climate and plant and animal life as well as to the development of its Native American population.[2] Webb's study in and of itself is a monument to historical scholarship. It may have reinforced, however, the tendency in western scholarship to stress regional uniqueness, often within a Turnerian context.

When placed in the superficial-fundamental change perspective of this book, it could be argued that much of what Webb described as change unique to the Plains was actually only superficial change. It could be further argued that the history of the Great Plains agricultural settlement is actually one of continuity. This proposition becomes clearer when change is comparatively studied in terms of Native American and white settlement in the Plains.

The development of a composite Plains Indian culture is a story of fundamental change resulting from the adaptation of traditional practices to new environmental conditions. The Native American Plains population was composed of thirty different peoples representing six language stocks. By 1860 their culture came to represent two-thirds of the Native Americans. When hunting and gathering people from the West and agricultural people from the East gathered on the Plains, gross cultural differences existed between them. Yet by 1800 many of these differences had disappeared.[3]

Of all the environmental variables on the Plains, the buffalo had the most immediate impact on the Indians who migrated to the region. Aside from the obvious economic transformation, the buffalo's migration patterns fundamentally altered political and social structures of Native Americans. The buffalo gathered in mass herds during the summer breeding season, and afterwards dispersed into smaller herds of approximately twenty animals to begin a seasonal migration that ranged from 200 to 400 miles. Adaptation to this buffalo migration pattern resulted in profound changes

92

in long-standing institutions and beliefs. For example, those tribes who came from the East brought with them complex kinship systems; those who migrated from the West brought much simpler kinship systems. The Plains environment effected an amalgamation process in which western tribes took on more complex social systems while those of the East were simplified. Both groups of Native Americans evolved a similar camp and band organization that suited the migration pattern of the buffaloes.[4] One anthropologist succinctly describes this process as one in which the Cheyenne, a sedentary and agricultural people, were isolated from their traditions and consequently were transformed by the Plains environment into "a race of nomad and predatory hunters, with such entire change of habit and ceremony that the old life is remembered only in sacred tradition."[5]

The political, social, and economic transformation of the Plains Indians destroyed the cohesiveness characteristic of older and more established societies. With the erosion of established institutions and the resultant loss of cohesiveness, an identity crisis emerged in their culture. Much like the process that characterized change and the resultant identity crisis among Europeans in colonial America and Americans in the early nineteenth century, new institutions evolved in Plains culture to fill the need for unity and stability. Scholars suggest that the social and military associations so common to Plains culture were an adaptive response to the loss of older kinship systems. The Cheyenne for example had six military societies, each performing specific and different functions but sharing the common

function of providing a new hierarchial system for iden-
tifying and ranking people.[6] The replacement of older
kinship systems with sodalities was an example of fundamental change.

Other scholars point to the ritualism associated with
Plains Indian warfare as a unity-producing institution.
The function of ritual in Native American culture did
not change, of course, but its specific focus did. Plains
Indian warfare placed greater emphasis on strategy and
cunning than on killing. For example touching one's
enemy in his sleep without being detected would be
considered a much higher achievement than merely
killing him. The emphasis on warfare, in whatever context, affected definitions of merit. One finds an erosion
of hereditary merit and the evolution of merit through
achievement. Consequently, Plains Indian cultures
placed greater stress on youth, masculinity, and cour-
age as guidelines for ranking and identification. The
erosion of hereditary merit coincided also with the rise
of material acquisition as a measure of rank. The number of wives and horses one possessed, for example, was
extremely important in positioning people in Plains Indian culture.

The creation of a composite Plains Indian culture of
course was not a cognitive process. It was simply a matter of cultural ecology. Plains Indians did not possess
the technology to overcome environmental obstacles
to the continuation of economic, political, and social
patterns. The result was fundamental change as a result
of having to adapt to the demands of the environment.

The story of white agricultural settlement of the

Plains is just the opposite. New technology allowed the white man to temporarily overcome environmental obstacles to existing economic, political, and social practices. Dry farming, new strains of wheat, and new milling techniques—along with the extension of the railroad—made agriculture on the Plains a tenable proposition. Advances in technology also overcame environmental obstacles such as the shortage of water and wood. Barbed wire, deep wells, windmills, and a plethora of inventions in the agricultural implements industry have all been seen as short-run technological triumphs over environmental obstacles.[7]

American agriculture had advanced beyond the subsistence stage when the Plains were settled. As a specialized industry Great Plains agriculture was concerned with the national and international marketplace. The farmer was a rural businessman who stood alongside the banker, industrialist, and land speculator in his concern with matters of capitalization, credit, production, competition, and marketing. Those obstacles that did exist to threaten existing practices were not part of the Plains environment but part of national monetary policies and the ramifications of industrialization. The farmer faced these obstacles in common with other businessmen, and in time his response to these trends was similar.

New machinery, for example, simultaneously furthered the indebtedness of the farmer and increased his production, consequently lowering the price of his produce. Eastern industrialists and ranchers responded to the new demands of a marketplace economy by orga-

95

nizing into trade associations that were designed to promote efficiency, lessen harmful competition, standardize procedures, and generally more effectively manipulate the variables involved in producing and marketing goods. Farmers, although not so quickly, responded in much the same fashion. The Grange, Farmer's Alliance, and Farmer's Union clearly were western manifestations of this same impulse. Farmers—long the bastions of individualism—began to see this approach as the only way to survive. Several tangible elements made them aware of this reality. Farmers perceived their problems in terms of the monopolistic hold that granaries and railroads had on them. These observable institutions came to symbolize the fact that the interests of the eastern industrialist were not those of the agriculturalist.[8] Newt Gresham, the organizer of the Farmer's Union, was well aware of these business realities when he stated that the Union's purpose was to "assist our members in buying and selling, to educate the agricultural class in scientific farming, . . . to systematize methods of production and distribution . . . to bring farmers up to the standards of other industries and business enterprises."[9]

The subtreasury plan in its various forms from 1889 to 1892 most clearly exemplifies a comprehensive attempt to manipulate the agricultural marketplace. According to the plan, the government was to build warehouses in which farmers could store their harvest. This, in turn, would have allowed the government to control the outflow of produce and consequently to effect a higher price at the time of sale. The farmer, upon depositing his crop, would receive immediate payment for eighty per cent of the crop's market value which he could use to reduce his indebtedness. The subtreasury plan would have simultaneously addressed all of the farmer's capitalization, credit, currency, and production problems and would have made him a more effective competitor on the open marketplace.

Technology, while paving the way for Great Plains agriculture, at the same time linked that region to the nation, links that assured political, social, and economic continuity and discouraged fundamental change unique to the region. Farmers, ranchers, and businessmen were a part of the same historical process and this process should concern western historians as much as regional uniqueness.

Notes

PREFACE

1. The contest between man and environment, of course, is not a new research endeavor. Anthropologists and geographers have been concerned with this interaction since the inception of their disciplines. Even historians, and Frederick Jackson Turner is an example, have been aware of this process.

Cultural ecology, a presently developing field of interest in geography and anthropology, has a direct interest in cultural and environmental interaction. For a good overview of this field and an extensive bibliography, see Robert McC. Netting, "The Ecological Approach in Cultural Study," (Addison-Wesley Modular Publication no. 6, 1971). Cultural ecology invariably has an evolutionary perspective, and there are three distinct schools. The Unilinear school proceeds from the assumption that all societies evolve through similar and detectable stages. This school is best represented by Leslie White, *The Science of Culture.* The Cultural Relativist views each society as a separate entity and hence is concerned with uniqueness. This view is usually associated with the work of Ruth Benedict, *Patterns of Culture.* Finally, the Multilinear school assumes that basic culture types may develop similarly under similar circumstances. This school rejects the rigidity of stages and looks to similar culture types as manifesting themselves at different rates and in different ways. The best representative study of the school is Julian Steward, *Theory of Culture Change: The Methodology of Multilinear Evolution.* Some scholars dismiss evolution entirely as a method of studying culture. Bronislaw Malinowski, *A Scientific Theory of Culture,* studies culture as a static phenomenon and almost totally rejects regularities and patterns in cultural developments.

Cultural ecology as a subfield of geography shares most of its methodological concerns with anthropology. For a good overview of cultural ecology in geography see the introduction in Marvin W. Mikesell and Philip L. Wagner, eds., *Readings in Cultural Geography.* In the same volume see also Derwent Whittlesey, "Major Agricultural Regions of the Earth" and Max Sorre's essay, "The Concept of *Genre De Vie.*" Another volume that should be useful to the frontier scholar is William L. Thomas, Jr., ed., *Man's Role in Changing the Face of the Earth.* A number of essays in this book are methodologically if not topically useful to the American historian. A classic essay in this work is Alexander Spoehr, "Cultural Differences in the Interpretations of Natural Resources." Also see E. Estyn Evans, "The Ecology of Peasant Life in Western Europe," and Gottfried Pfiefer, "The Quality of Land Use of Tropical Cultivators." A number of geographers are directly concerned with comparative American frontier studies. Most historians are familiar with Marvin Mikesell's "Comparative Studies in Frontier History," *Annals, Association of American Geographers* 51 (1961): 62–74. For a good overview of geographical models for frontier study, see John Hudson, "Theory and Methodology in Comparative Frontier Studies" in David H. Miller and Jerome O. Steffen, eds., *Frontiers: A Comparative Approach.*

CHAPTER 1

1. Frederick Jackson Turner, "The Significance of the Frontier in American History," *American Historical Association Annual Report for the Year 1893,* p. 199. This discussion of the cis-Mississippi farming frontier is concerned with agricultural settlement north of the Ohio River from the colonial period to the eve of the Civil War.

2. Frederick Jackson Turner, "The West and American Ideals," an address delivered at the University of Washington, June 17, 1914, *Washington Historical Quarterly* 5 (October 1914): 243–57.

3. Ray Allen Billington, *America's Frontier Heritage,* p. 15.

4. Walter Prescott Webb, *The Great Frontier.*

5. Webb develops the 400-year boom hypothesis in chapter 1 of *The Great Frontier.*

6. Walter Prescott Webb, "The Western World Frontier," in Walker D. Wyman and Clifton B. Kroeber, eds., *The Frontier in Perspective,* p. 113.

7. Billington, *America's Frontier Heritage,* p. 25.

8. Ibid.

9. See note 1 of the preface.

10. For a good discussion of the application of Freudian models to American character see Walter Metzger, "Generalizations about National Character: An Analytical Essay," in Louis Gottschalk, ed., *Generalization in the Writing of History;* and David M. Potter, *People of Plenty: Economic Abundance and American Character,* chapter 2. Those works of Sigmund Freud that have the most direct historical application are *Three Essays on the Theory of Sexuality; Civilization and its Discontents: The Ego and the Id;* and *Inhibitions, Symptoms and Anxiety.* Freud made some attempt to deal with collective behavior in *Group Psychology and the Analysis of the Ego* (International Psycho-Analytical Library, 1922). For adaptations of Freud to group behavior see Abram Kardiner et al, *The Psychological Frontiers of Society;* and Abram Kardiner, *The Psychodynamics of Primitive Social Organization.* A useful companion work that assists in understanding Kardiner's theory of "basic personality" is Ralph Linton, *The Cultural Background of Personality.*

A fuller development of psychological social character studies can be found in Erich Fromm, *Escape from Freedom; Man for Himself: An Inquiry into the Psychology of Ethics;* and "Individual and Social Origins of Neurosis" in Clyde Kluckhohn and Henry A. Murray, eds., *Personality in Nature, Society and Culture.* Difficult to classify but closely related Freudian anthropological inquiries include Margaret Mead, *And Keep Your Powder Dry;* and her essay, "The Study of National Character," in Daniel Lerner, ed.,

The Policy Sciences: Recent Developments in Scope and Method.
Mead's work—here as elsewhere—deals with generational erosion
of cultural traits and its impact on personality.

11. All of Erikson's works are germane to historical inquiry, but
of particular interest are *Childhood and Society, Identity Youth
and Crisis,* and *Youth: Change and Challenge.*

12. Erik Erikson, "Youth: Fidelity and Diversity," *Daedalus: Journal of the American Academy of Arts and Sciences,* 91 (Winter
1962): 6–7.

13. Riesman's work is carefully scrutinized in Seymour Martin
Lipset and Leo Lowenthal, eds., *Culture and Society: The Work
of David Riesman Reviewed.* Also see Riesman's "Psychological
Types and National Character," *American Quarterly* 5 (Winter
1953): 325–43.

14. David Riesman, "From Morality to Morale," in Alfred H.
Stanton and Stewart E. Perry, eds., *Personality and Political Crisis,
New Perspectives from Social Science and Psychiatry for the Study
of War and Politics,* pp. 83–84. This essay is a succinct discussion
of themes developed in *The Lonely Crowd.*

15. Riesman, "Morality to Morale," pp. 85–87.

16. These accounts are numerous and vary in quality. The most
useful and widely read observations are those of Charles Dickens,
American Notes; Harriet Martineau, *Society in America;* Frances
Trollope, *Domestic Manners of the Americans;* Michel Chevalier,
Society, Manners and Politics in the United States; Lord James
Bryce, *The American Commonwealth.* Other accounts not so widely
known but equally useful are Edward S. Abdy, *Journal of a Residence and Town in the United States,* 3 vols. (London, J. Murray,
1835); Bernhard, Duke of Saxe-Weimar Eisenbach, *Travels through
North America 1825 and 1826,* 2 vols. (Philadelphia, Carey, Lea &
Blanchard, 1828); John Eyre, *The European Stranger in America*
(New York, 1839); Francis Grund, *Aristocracy in America* (London,
R. Bentley, 1839); Joseph Pickering, *Inquiries of an Emigrant* (London, E. Wilson, 1832). Scholarly efforts to review European observations of America can be found in Allan Nevins, ed., *America
through British Eyes;* Jane Louise Mesick, *The English Traveller
in America, 1785–1835;* Max Berger, *The British Traveller in Amer-*

ica, 1836–1860 (New York, Columbia University Press, 1943); Henry Steele Commager, ed., *America in Perspective: The United States through Foreign Eyes* (New York, Random House, 1947); and Marvin Fisher, *Workshops in the Wilderness: The European Response to American Industrialization, 1830–1860.* Of all the European accounts, Alexis de Tocqueville's *Democracy in America* is perhaps the most widely known. There are useful criticisms and discussions of Tocqueville's work in George W. Pierson, *Tocqueville and Beaumont in America;* Seymour Drescher, "Tocqueville's Two Democracies," *Journal of the History of Ideas* 25 (April-June 1964): 201–16; Edward T. Gargean, "Tocqueville and the Problem of Historical Prognosis," *American Historical Review* 68 (January 1963): 332–45; Jack Lively, *The Social and Political Thought of Alexis de Tocqueville;* J. P. Mayer, *Prophet of the Mass Age: A Study of Alexis de Tocqueville* (London, J. M. Dent & Sons, Ltd., 1939); Marvin Zetterbaum, *Tocqueville and the Problem of Democracy.*

17. Alexis de Tocqueville, *Democracy in America,* ed. Philip Bradley (New York, Vintage Press, 1945), p. 11.

18. Stanley Elkins and Eric McKitrick, "A Meaning for Turner's Frontier: Part I, Democracy in the Old Northwest," *Political Science Quarterly* 69 (September 1954): 327.

19. Ibid., p. 328.

20. Ibid., p. 329.

21. Ibid., p. 330.

22. Kenneth Lockridge, *A New England Town: The First Hundred Years, Dedham, Massachusetts, 1636–1736.* Lockridge is part of a school of colonial historians that has effectively incorporated demographic methods in its work. Also see John Demos, *A Little Commonwealth: Family Life in Plymouth Colony* and Philip J. Greven, *Four Generations: Population, Land and Family in Andover, Massachusetts.*

23. Bernard Bailyn, "Political Experience and Enlightenment Ideals in Eighteenth Century America," *American Historical Review* 67 (January, 1962), p. 351.

24. Gordon Wood, *The Creation of the American Republic, 1776–1787,* p. 476.

25. John William Ward, *Andrew Jackson: Symbol for an Age.*

26. Ibid., p. 209.

27. Ibid., p. 51.

28. For a good discussion on the development of American education see Ruth Elson, "American Schoolbooks and 'Culture' in the Nineteenth Century," *Mississippi Valley Historical Review* 46 (December 1959): 413, and, by the same author, in *Guardians of Tradition: American Schoolbooks of the Nineteenth Century.*

29. Alan Heimert, *Religion and the American Mind, From the Great Awakening to the Revolution,* p. 14.

30. Philip Schaff, *America: A Sketch of its Political, Social and Religious Character,* p. 104.

31. These passages from Schaff's *America* were taken from Sidney Mead, *The Lively Experiment: The Shaping of Christianity in America.*

32. James Willard Hurst, *Law and the Conditions of Freedom in the Nineteenth Century United States,* pp. 5–6.

33. Ibid., pp. 14–18, 48–90.

34. The best studies of banking in the Jacksonian period are Bray Hammond, *Banks and Politics in America from the Revolution to the Civil War,* and Robert Remini, *Andrew Jackson and the Bank War.* Studies of the rise of the small capitalist are usually associated with Richard Hofstadter's essay, "Andrew Jackson and the Rise of Liberal Capitalism," in his book *The American Political Tradition and the Men Who Made It* and Marvin Meyers, *Jacksonian Persuasion: Politics & Beliefs.* The best historiographic literature on the Jacksonian period include Alfred A. Cave, *Jacksonian Democracy and the Historians;* Charles G. Sellars, Jr., "Andrew Jackson versus the Historians," *Mississippi Valley Historical Review* 44 (March 1958): 615–34; and the bibliographic essay in Edward Pessen, *Jacksonian America: Society, Personality, and Politics.*

35. Stuart Weems Bruchey, *The Roots of American Economic Growth 1608–1861: An Essay on Social Causation,* p. 209.

36. Percy W. Bidwell and John I. Falconer, *History of Agriculture in the Northern United States, 1620–1860,* p. 163. Also see Morris Birkbeck, *Letters from Illinois* and George Flower, *History of the English Settlement in Edwards County, Illinois.*

37. Bidwell and Falconer, *History of Agriculture,* p. 164.

104

38. Ibid., p. 255.
39. Paul W. Gates, *The Farmer's Age: Agriculture 1815–1860,* pp. 312–27. There is also an excellent bibliography in the Gates' volume. To place agriculture in a national economic perspective, see Louis Bernard Schmidt's excellent article, "Internal Commerce and the Development of National Economy before 1860," *The Journal of Political Economy* 47 (August 1939): 798–822.
40. John Peck, *A Guide for Emigrants, Containing Sketches of Illinois, Missouri, and the Adjacent Parts,* originally published in 1831.
41. Bidwell and Falconer, *History of Agriculture,* pp. 263, 265.
42. Caroline Kirkland, *A New Home, Who'll Follow? Glimpses of Western Life,* p. 72.

CHAPTER 2

1. The most complete and respected work on mercantilism is Eli Heckscher, *Mercantilism.* Also see G. Schmoller, *The Mercantile System and its Historical Significance;* Charles H. Wilson, *Mercantilism;* and Peter King, *The Development of the English Economy to 1750.* For a reliable review of the historiographical development of the subject, see D. C. Coleman, ed., *Revisions in Mercantilism.* Some insight can be gained on the relationship between national policy and trading practices in Barry Supple, *Commercial Crisis and Change in England, 1600–1642;* C. H. Wilson, *England's Apprenticeship, 1603–1763;* and Murray Lawson, *Fur: A Study in English Mercantilism 1700–1775.* University of Toronto Studies in History and Economics, no. 9 (Toronto, 1943).
2. N. S. B. Gras, *Business and Capitalism: An Introduction to Business History,* pp. 74–90.
3. William Clark Kennerly as told to Elizabeth Russell, *Persimmon Hill: A Narrative of Old St. Louis and the Far West,* p. 8.
4. William Appleman Williams, "The Age of Mercantilism: An Interpretation of the American Political Economy, 1763 to 1828," *William and Mary Quarterly* 15 (October 1958): 419–20.
5. William Clark to George Rogers Clark, September 24, 1806,

Comparative Frontiers

in Reuben Gold Thwaites, ed., *Original Journals of the Lewis and Clark Expedition, 1804–1806*, 7: 338–39.

6. The best treatment of the Hudson's Bay Company is E. E. Rich, *The History of the Hudson's Bay Company, 1607–1807*. For studies of a general nature, see H. A. Innis, *The Fur Trade in Canada* and Frederick Merk, ed., *Fur Trade and Empire, George L. Simpson's Journal;* the introduction to Richard Glover, *David Thompson's Narrative, 1784–1812,* and John S. Galbraith, "British American Competition in the Border Fur Trade of the 1820's," *Minnesota History* 40 (Winter 1966), and K. G. Davis, "From Competition to Union," *Minnesota History* 40 (Winter 1966): 241–49.

7. The standard text on the factory system is Ora Peake, *The American Factory System, 1796–1822.* Also useful is Edgar B. Wesley, "The Government Factory System Among the Indians, 1795-1822," *Journal of Economics and Business History* 4 (May 1932): 487–511; and Larry A. McFarlane, "Economic Theories Significant in the Rise of the United States Indian Factory System, 1795–1817" (Master's thesis, University of Missouri, 1955).

8. Thomas Jefferson to Chastellux, June 7, 1785, *Papers of Thomas Jefferson,* ed. Julian P. Boyd et al., 18 vols. (Princeton: Princeton University Press, 1950–1971), 8: 185–86.

9. There is considerable debate on the subject of Jeffersonian Indian Policy. For an understanding of Jeffersonian Indian Policy several works are indispensable. See Francis Paul Prucha, *American Indian Policy in the Formative Years: The Indian Trade and Intercourse Acts, 1790–1834;* and the following three works by Reginald Horsman: "Indian Policy in the Northwest," *William and Mary Quarterly* 18 (January 1961): 35–53; *Expansion and the American Indian Policy, 1783–1812;* and "American Indian Policy and the Origins of Manifest Destiny," *University of Birmingham Historical Journal* 11 (December 1968): 128–40. See also Jerome O. Steffen, *William Clark: Jeffersonian Man on the Frontier* and Bernard W. Sheehan, *Seeds of Extinction: Jeffersonian Philanthropy and the American Indian.*

10. William Clark to Secretary of War, November 20, 1831, Clark Papers, 4, Kansas State Historical Society, Topeka, Kansas. The career of others influential in national Indian and trade policies might be profitably explained with this framework in mind.

11. William Clark to Secretary of War, October 1, 1815, *American State Papers: Indian Affairs,* 1: 77–78.

12. Gras, *Business and Capitalism,* pp. 81–88, 103–14.

13. Ibid., 88–103.

14. For an excellent biography of Manuel Lisa see Richard Oglesby, *Manuel Lisa and the Opening of the Missouri Fur Trade.*

15. St. Louis Missouri Fur Company Ledger Book, 1809–1814, Missouri Historical Society-Jefferson Memorial, St. Louis. Although there is no complete study of the Missouri Fur Company, useful sources on the subject are Richard Oglesby, *Manuel Lisa and the Opening of the Missouri Fur Trade;* Hiram Chittenden, *The American Fur Trade of the Far West;* and Paul C. Phillips, *History of the American Fur Trade.*

16. Oglesby, *Manuel Lisa,* pp. 126–49.

17. Ibid., 150–78.

18. Besides the general studies of the fur trade already noted, see Kenneth W. Porter, *John Jacob Astor: Business Man.* Also useful is Washington Irving, *Astoria.*

19. I gathered the prosopographic material mainly from Leroy Hafen, *The Mountain Men and the Fur Trade of the Far West.*

20. Hafen, *Mountain Men,* 9: 125–31, 3: 221–28. See also J. Ward Ruckman, "Ramsay Crooks and the Fur Trade of the Northwest," *Minnesota History* 7 (March 1926): 18–31 and David Lavender, *The Fist in the Wilderness.*

21. Hafen, *Mountain Men,* 6: 185–206. See also T. C. Elliot, "Wilson Price Hunt, 1723–1842," *Oregon Historical Quarterly* 32 (1913): 130–34.

22. Hafen, *Mountain Men,* 5: 227–38, also see Jean C. Nielson, "Donald McKenzie in the Snake Country Fur Trade, 1816–18," *Pacific Northwest Quarterly* 31: 161–79, and Cecil W. MacKenzie, *Donald McKenzie: King of the Northwest.*

23. Hafen, *Mountain Men,* 9: 361–64, also see Phillip Ashton Rollins, *The Discovery of the Oregon Trail: Robert Stuart's Narratives.*

24. William H. Goetzmann, "The Mountain Man as Jacksonian Man," *American Quarterly* 15 (Fall 1963): 404–405.

25. Ibid., p. 409. The phrase "expectant capitalist" was originally used by Richard Hofstader in his discussion of Jacksonian Democracy in *The American Political Tradition and the Men Who Made It.*

26. Goetzmann, "Mountain Man," p. 410.

27. Harvey Lewis Carter and Marcia Carpenter Spencer, "Stereotypes of the Mountain Man," *Western Historical Quarterly* 6 (January 1975): 24.

28. Ibid., p. 25.

29. Ibid., p. 26.

30. For William Goetzmann's reply to the Carter and Spencer article, see the Communications sections of the *Western Historical Quarterly* 6 (July 1975): 295–300. Carter's reply to Goetzmann is in the same issue of the *Western Historical Quarterly* at pp. 301–302.

CHAPTER 3

1. John E. Rouse, *Cattle of North America,* World Cattle, vol. 3, pp. 487–88.

2. Ibid., pp. 488–89. Charles Wayland Towne and Edward Norris Wentworth, *Cattle and Men,* pp. 130–47.

3. Lewis Gray, *History of Agriculture in the Southern United States to 1860,* p. 151.

4. Towne & Wentworth, *Cattle and Men,* p. 145.

5. The Ohio Valley ranching industry is covered quite adequately in Paul Henlein, *The Cattle Kingdom in the Ohio Valley,* and, by the same author, in "Early Cattle Ranches of the Ohio Valley," *Agricultural History* 35 (July 1961): 150–54.

6. For a discussion of the Spanish influence on American ranching see Odie B. Faulk, "Ranching in Spanish Texas," *Hispanic American Historical Review* 45 (May 1965): 257–66; Sandra L. Myers, "The Ranching Frontier: Spanish Institutional Backgrounds of the Plains Cattle Industry," in Harold M. Hollingsworth, ed., *Essays on the American West* (Austin: University of Texas Press, 1959); William H. Dusenberry, *The Mexican Mesta: The Administration of Ranching in Colonial Mexico;* Terry G. Jordan, "The Origin of Anglo-American Cattle Ranching in Texas: A Documentation of Diffusion from the Lower South," *Economic Geography* 45 (January 1969): 63–87, and, by the same author, "The Origin and Distribution of Open-Range

Cattle Ranching," *Social Science Quarterly* 53 (June 1972): 103–21.

7. Towne & Wentworth, *Cattle and Men,* pp. 157–58; also see Herbert O. Brayer, *Life of Tom Candy Ponting: An Autobiography.*

8. Joe B. Frantz, *Gail Bordon: Dairyman to a Nation,* pp. 195–221.

9. Tom Lea, *The King Ranch,* 1: 154.

10. The best general works on the development of the range cattle industry are Lewis Atherton, *The Cattle Kings;* Lewis Pelzer, *The Cattlemen's Frontier: A Record of the Trans-Mississippi Cattle Industry, 1850–1890;* and Ernest Osgood, *The Day of the Cattleman.* These three works should be supplemented by Edward Everett Dale, *The Range Cattle Industry: Ranching on the Great Plains from 1865 to 1925* and Joseph G. McCoy, *Historic Sketches of the Cattle Trade of the West and Southwest.* The most useful existing works on cattle trailing are Jimmy M. Skaggs, *The Cattle Trailing Industry: Between Supply and Demand, 1866–1890* and Wayne Gard, *The Chisholm Trail.* On cattle towns, by far the best study is Robert R. Dykstra, *The Cattle Towns.*

11. The standard treatment of Richard King is in Tom Lea, *The King Ranch.*

12. An existing biography of George Littlefield is J. Evetts Haley, *George Littlefield, Texan;* however, a more scholarly treatment of Littlefield is David B. Gracy II, "George Washington Littlefield: Portrait of a Cattleman," *Southwestern Historical Quarterly* 68 (October 1964): 237–39 and, by the same author, "George W. Littlefield: From Cattle to Colonization, 1871–1920," in John A. Carroll, ed., *Reflections of Western Historians* (Tucson, University of Arizona Press, 1969).

13. While John Iliff still awaits a biographer, the most useful information on him can be found in Maurice Frink et al., *When Grass Was King: Contribution to the Western Cattle Industry Study,* and Ora Peake, *The Colorado Range Cattle Industry.*

14. An existing biography of Goodnight is J. Evetts Haley, *Charles Goodnight: Cowman and Plainsman.*

15. There is no existent biography of Nelson Story. A sketch of his life appears in *The Rocky Mountain Husbandman,* May 5, 1938, and an account of his career written by his son Byron Story is contained in the Archives in Western History, University of Wyoming, Laramie.

16. Atherton, *The Cattle Kings,* p. 219. In addition to the afore-mentioned sources on King, Goodnight, Littlefield, Iliff, and Story, Atherton should be consulted because his use of the available data on these individuals presents a perceptive conceptual framework not found in the existing biographies.

17. For other examples of this kind of literature, see Walter Baron Von Richtofen, *Cattle Raising on the Plains of North America;* James MacDonald, *Food from the Far West;* and William A. Baille-Grohman, *Camps in the Rockies.*

18. It is impossible to cover all of the sources on the northward spread of the cattle industry; however, a few of the most useful are Orin J. Oliphant, *On the Cattle Ranges of the Oregon Country;* Harold E. Briggs, *Frontiers of the Northwest;* idem, "The Development and Decline of Open Range Ranching in the Northwest," *Mississippi Valley Historical Review* 20 (March 1934): 521–36; Robert G. Athearn, *High Country Empire: The High Plains and the Rockies;* Ora Peake, *The Colorado Range Cattle Industry;* T. A. Larson, *History of Wyoming;* Robert H. Fletcher, *From Grass to Fences: The Montana Range Cattle Story;* Bob Lee and Dick Williams, *Last Grass Frontier: The South Dakota Stock Grower Heritage.*

19. There are several good accounts which cover foreign and domestic investment patterns in the later ranching era. See Gene M. Gressley, *Bankers and Cattlemen* and, by the same author, "Broker to the British: Francis Smith and Company," *Southwestern Historical Quarterly* 71 (July 1967): 7–25; W. Turrentine Jackson, *The Enterprising Scot: Investors in the American West after 1873;* Maurice Frink et al., *When Grass was King: Contributions to the Western Range Cattle Industry Study;* Richard Graham, "The Investment Boom in British-Texan Cattle Companies, 1800–1885," *Business History Review* 34 (Winter 1960): 421–45; William W. Savage, Jr., "Cows and Englishmen: Observations on Investment by British Immigrants in the Western Range Cattle Industry," *Red River Valley Historical Review* 1 (Spring 1974): 34–45; and, by the same author, "Plunkett of the EK: Irish Notes on the Wyoming Cattle Industry in the 1880s," *Annals of Wyoming* 43 (Fall 1971): 205–14.

20. Alfred D. Chandler, "The Beginning of 'Big Business' in American Industry," *The Business History Review* 33 (Spring 1959): 1–31.

Also by the same author see *Strategy and Structure: Chapters in the History of the Industrial Enterprise.* In addition, a useful conceptual reference can be found in Thomas C. Cochran and William Miller, *The Age of Enterprise: A Social History of Industrial America* and by Thomas Cochran, *Business in American Life.*

21. Chandler, "The Beginnings of 'Big Business,'" p. 26.

22. Ibid., p. 28.

23. Some of the existing histories of the stock growers' associations are Maurice Frink, *Cow Country Cavalcade: Eighty Years of the Wyoming Stock Growers' Association;* W. Turrentine Jackson, "The Wyoming Stock Growers' Association; Political Power in Wyoming Territory, 1873–1890," *Mississippi Valley Historical Review* 33 (March 1947): 571–94 and, by the same author, "The Wyoming Stock Growers' Association: Its Years of Temporary Decline, 1886–1890," *Agricultural History* 22 (October 1948): 260–70. See also John R. Burroughs, *Guardian of the Grasslands: The First Hundred Years of the Wyoming Stock Growers' Association.* The Colorado Stock Growers' Association is covered in Ora Peake, *The Colorado Range Cattle Industry,* while the Montana Stockman's Association is treated in Robert H. Fletcher, *From Grass to Fences: The Montana Range Cattle Story.* The Texas and Southwestern Cattle Raisers' Association is covered in Lewis Nordyke, *The Great Roundup: The Story of Texas and Southwestern Cattlemen.*

24. Some existing ranching histories are Harley T. Burton, *History of the JA Ranch;* William C. Holden, *The Spur Ranch;* and Lewis Nordyke, *Cattle Empire: The Fabulous History of the 3,000,-000 Acre XIT.* A more useful study of the XIT is David B. Gracy II, *Littlefield Lands: Colonization on the Texas Plains, 1912–1920.* Also see A. Ray Stephens, *The Taft Ranch: A Texas Principality,* and Dulcie Sullivan, *The LS Brand: The Story of a Texas Panhandle Ranch.* For land and cattle company histories, see Virginia H. Taylor, *The Franco-Texan Land Company;* W. M. Pearce, *The Matador Land and Cattle Company;* Lester F. Sheffy, *The Francklyn Land and Cattle Company;* Harmon R. Mothershead, *The Swan Land and Cattle Company, LTD;* and William W. Savage, Jr., *The Cherokee Strip Live Stock Association: Federal Regulation and the Cattleman's Last Frontier.*

25. There is one exception to the trend of continuity in western range history—cowboy mythology. The cowboy cult and the code of the west has become a significant and lasting part of American popular culture. But even this subject has gained its relevancy in recent years from the perspective of an industrial society and its receptiveness to cowboy mythology. The best works on this subject are David Brion Davis, "Ten Gallon Hero," *American Quarterly* 6 (Summer 1954): 111–25; William W. Savage, Jr., ed., *Cowboy Life: Reconstructing an American Myth,* and, by the same author, "The Cowboy: A Comment," in *The Cowboy: Six-Shooters, Songs and Sex,* ed. Charles W. Harris and Buck Rainey, pp. 154–63.

26. Atherton, *The Cattle Kings,* pp. 59–61, 63.

27. Ibid., pp. 65, 88–89. More information on Kohrs can be found in Larry Gill, "From Butcher to Beef King: Conrad Kohrs," in *Cowboys and Cattlemen,* ed. Michael S. Kennedy.

28. Useful sources on the subject are Edward C. Kirkland, *Dream and Thought in the Business Community;* Robert McCloskey, *American Conservatism in the Age of Enterprise;* Irvin Wyllie, *Self-Made Man in America;* and Sigmund Diamond, *The Reputation of the American Businessman.*

CHAPTER 4

1. The most widely accepted definition of the frontier stage of mining is presented by Rodman Paul in *Mining Frontiers of the Far West, 1848–1880.* Paul associated the mining frontier with the placer stage of gold mining. Paul's succinct study is an excellent beginning point for students of the far western mining frontier. Another usable general study is William S. Greever, *The Bonanza West: The Story of the Western Rushes, 1848–1900.*

2. Charles Shinn, *Mining Camps: A Study in American Frontier Government,* p. 110.

3. For an excellent comparison of American and British mining frontiers in the Fraser River region of Oregon see William J. Trimble, *The Mining Advance into the Inland Empire: . . .* University of

Wisconsin History Series, bulletin no. 638, vol. 3 no. 2 (Madison, 1914).

4. Duane A. Smith, *Rocky Mountain Mining Camps: The Urban Frontier,* p. 47.

5. Paul, *Mining Frontiers,* p. 7.

6. The general question of indigenous versus imported mining practices is treated in Otis Young, *Western Mining: An Informal Account of Precious Metals Prospecting, Placering, Lode Mining and Milling on the American Frontier from Spanish Times to 1893* (Norman: University of Oklahoma Press, 1970), also by the same author, *How They Dug Gold: An Informal History of Frontier Prospecting, Placering, Lode-Mining and Milling in Arizona and the Southwest* (Tucson, 1967). See also Otis Young's article "The Spanish Tradition in Gold and Silver Mining," *Arizona and the West* (Winter 1965). Also useful are Thomas Rickard, *A History of American Mining* and Clark Spence, *Mining Engineers & the American West—the Lace Boot Brigade, 1849–1933.* Finally, an international comparison should begin with W. P. Morrell, *The Gold Rushes;* H. C. Allen, *Bush and Backwoods;* and Jay Monaghan, *Australians and the Gold Rush.*

7. Thomas A. Rickard, *A History of American Mining,* p. 33.

8. Fletcher Green, "Georgia's Forgotten Industry: Gold," *The Georgia Historical Quarterly* 19 (June 1935): 98–100; T. Conn Bryan, "The Gold Rush in Georgia," *Georgia Review* 9 (Winter 1955): 398–99.

9. Green, "Georgia's Forgotten Industry," pp. 101–106.

10. E. Merton Coulter, *Auraria, The Story of a Georgia Gold-Mining Town,* pp. 17–31.

11. Green, "Georgia's Forgotten Industry," p. 109.

12. Coulter, *Auraria,* p. 20.

13. Lewis Gray, *History of Agriculture in the Southern United States to 1800,* 2: 1039; *DeBows Review: The Commercial Review of the South and West . . .* 1 (1846): 44.

14. Coulter, *Auraria,* pp. 33–46.

15. William Gilmore Simms, *Guy Rivers: A Tale of Georgia . . .*

16. Coulter, *Auraria,* p. 55; taken from Mary C. Simms Oliphant et al., eds., *The Letters of William Gilmore Simms,* 1: 55.

17. Coulter, *Auraria,* pp. 73–93. For a comparative treatment of far western mining law and order see Duane A. Smith, *Rocky Mountain Mining Camps: The Urban Frontier.* See also Charles Shinn, *Mining Camps: A Study in American Frontier Government,* and Wayne Gard, *Frontier Justice* (Norman: University of Oklahoma Press, 1949). For local and regional treatments of this question, see the bibliographies in Rodman Paul, *Mining Frontiers of the Far West, 1848–1880,* and Ray Allen Billington, *Western Expansion: A History of the American Frontier,* 4th ed. (New York, Macmillan, 1974).

18. Coulter, *Auraria,* p. 58.

19. Bryan, "Gold Rush in Georgia," p. 400.

20. Green, "Georgia's Forgotten Industry," pp. 224–26; Bryan, "Gold Rush in Georgia," p. 402.

21. For a discussion of investment in far western mining, see Clark Spence, *British Investment and the American Mining Frontier, 1860–1901,* and W. Turrentine Jackson, *The Enterprising Scot: Investors in the American West after 1873.*

22. John Eagle to M. H. (Drum) Eagle, April 10, 1852. *John Eagle Papers, 1852–1855,* Huntington Library, San Marino, Calif.

23. Thomas Lewis to his wife, August 29, 1852, Thomas Lewis Journal and Letters, Western Americana Collection, Yale University.

24. George Cornell to his wife, January 1, 1853, George Cornell Journal, 1853, Western Americana Collection, Yale University.

25. Ibid.

26. Charles Pomeroy information found in Sarah M. (Aram) Cool Papers, 1850–1912, Huntington Library, San Marino, Calif.

27. George Applegate to Lewis M. Applegate, April 23, 1850, George Applegate Papers, Western Americana Collection, Yale University.

28. George Applegate Correspondence, October 8, 1851.

29. Ibid., February 25, 1852.

30. Sarah (Aram) Cool Papers 1850–1912, Huntington Library, San Marino, Calif.

31. William Swain to George Swain, November 14, 1850, William Swain Papers, Western Americana Collection, Yale University.

32. Harvey Lamb to Mother, September 15, 1852, Harvey Lamb Collection, Western Americana Collection, Yale University.
33. Thomas C. Lewis to wife, May 16, 1852, Thomas Lewis Journal and Letters, Western Americana Collection, Yale University.
34. Ibid., August 29, 1852.
35. Peter Cool Journal, 1851–1852, Huntington Library, San Marino, Calif.
36. Amos Pittman to Mother, May 2, 1852, Amos Pittman Papers, 1849–1853, Western Americana Collection, Yale University.
37. Ibid., July 28, 1853.

EPILOGUE

1. W. N. Davis, Jr., "Will the West Survive as a Field in American History," *Mississippi Valley Historical Review* 50 (March 1964): 685.
2. Webb, *The Great Plains*.
3. For a background in Native American cultures see Harold E. Driver, *Indians of North America;* A. L. Kroeber, *Anthropology, Race, Language, Culture, Psychology, Prehistory;* and Peter Farb, *Man's Rise to Civilization as Shown by the Indians of North America.*
4. For specialized studies of the Great Plains Native Americans, see George E. Hyde, *Indians of the High Plains* and Clark Wissler, *North American Indians of the Plains.* For the role of the buffalo in the formation of Plains Indian culture, see an early but still useful study, William T. Hornaday, *The Extermination of the American Bison with a Sketch of its Discovery and Life History.* See also Tom McHugh, *The Time of the Buffalo.*
5. Thomas Gladwin, "Personality Structure in the Plains," *Anthropological Quarterly* 30 (January 1957): 113.
6. Ibid., p. 115.
7. For general studies on the development of Great Plains agriculture see Webb, *The Great Plains;* Gilbert Fite, *The Farmer's Frontier, 1865–1900;* Fred A. Shannon, *The Farmer's Last Frontier;* and, also by Shannon, *An Appraisal of Walter Prescott Webb's*

The Great Plains: A Study in Institutions and Environment. Also of extreme importance is James C. Malin, *The Grassland of North America: Prolegomena to its History, with Addenda and Postscript.*

8. Useful works relating to the economic problems of late nineteenth-century agriculture are Lawrence Goodwyn, *The Democratic Promise: The Populist Moment in America;* John Hicks, *The Populist Revolt: A History of the Farmer's Alliance and the People's Party;* Theodore Saloutos, "The Agricultural Problem of the Late Nineteenth Century," *Agricultural History* 22 (March 1948): 156–74; and K. D. Bircha, "The Conservative Populists: A Hypothesis," *Agricultural History* 47 (January 1973): 9–24.

9. Theodore Saloutos, *Farmer Movements in the South,* p. 184.

Bibliography

ARCHIVAL MATERIAL

San Marino, California
  Henry Huntington Library
    1. Charles Penniman Daniels Papers
    2. John Eagle Papers, 1852–1855
    3. Peter Cool Journal, 1851–1852
    4. Sarah M. (Aram) Cool Papers, 1850–1912
New Haven, Connecticut
  Western Americana Collection
    1. Amos Pittman Papers, 1849–1853
    2. George Applegate Papers
    3. George Cornell Journal, 1853
    4. Harvey Lamb Collection
    5. Thomas Lewis Journal and Letters
    6. William Swain Papers
Topeka, Kansas
  Kansas State Historical Society
    William Clark Papers
    St. Louis, Missouri Fur Company Ledger Book, 1812–14
St. Louis, Missouri
  Missouri Historical Society-Jefferson Memorial
    William Clark Papers
    St. Louis, Missouri Fur Company Ledger Book, 1809–14

BOOKS

Allen, H. C. *Bush and Backwoods.* East Lansing: Michigan State University Press, 1959.

Athearn, Robert G. *High Country Empire: The High Plains and Rockies.* New York: McGraw-Hill, 1960.

Atherton, Lewis. *The Cattle Kings.* Bloomington: Indiana University Press, 1961.

Baille-Groham, William A. *Camps in the Rockies.* New York: Charles Scribner's Sons, 1882.

Benedict, Ruth. *Patterns of Culture.* New York: Houghton Mifflin Co., 1934.

Bidwell, Percy W. and Falconer, John I. *History of Agriculture in the Northern United States, 1620–1860.* Washington, D.C.: Carnegie Institution of Washington, 1925.

Billington, Ray Allen. *America's Frontier Heritage.* New York: Holt, Rinehart & Winston, 1966.

Birkbeck, Morris. *Letters from Illinois.* Introduction by Robert M. Sutton. New York: De Capo Press, 1970.

Brayer, Herbert O. *Life of Tom Candy Ponting: An Autobiography.* Evanston, Ill.: Branding Iron Press, 1952.

Briggs, Harold E. *Frontiers of the Northwest; A History of the Upper Missouri Valley.* New York: D. Appleton-Century Co., 1940.

Brisbin, James. *The Beef Bonanza or How to get Rich on the Plains.* Philadelphia: J. B. Lippincott & Co., 1881.

Bruchey, Stuart Weems. *The Roots of American Economic Growth 1608–1861: An Essay on Social Causation.* New York: Harper & Row, 1965.

Bryce, Lord James. *The American Commonwealth.* 2 vols. New York, Macmillan Co., 1888.

Burroughs, John R. *Guardian of the Grasslands: The First Hundred Years of the Wyoming Stock Growers' Association.* Cheyenne, Wyo.: Pioneer Print & Stationery Co., 1971.

Burton, Harley T. *History of the JA Ranch.* Austin: Texas Press of Von Boeckmann-Jones Co., 1928.

Cave, Alfred A. *Jacksonian Democracy and the Historians.* Gainsville: University of Florida Press, 1964.

Chandler, Alfred D. *Strategy and Structure: Chapters in the History of the Industrial Enterprise.* Cambridge, Mass.: M.I.T. Press, 1962.

Chevalier, Michel. *Society, Manners and Politics in the United States.* 1839. Edited by John William Ward. Garden City, N.Y.: Doubleday, 1961.

Chittenden, Hiram. *The American Fur Trade of the Far West.* 2 vols. New York: Press of the Pioneers, 1935.

Cochran, Thomas C. and Miller, William. *The Age of Enterprise: A Social History of Industrial America.* New York: Macmillan Co., 1942.

Cochran, Thomas. *Business in American Life.* New York: McGraw-Hill, 1972.

Coleman, D. C., ed. *Revisions in Mercantilism.* London: Methuen, 1969.

Coulter, E. Merton. *Auraria, The Story of a Georgia Gold-Mining Town.* Athens: University of Georgia Press, 1956.

Dale, Edward Everett. *The Range Cattle Industry: Ranching on the Great Plains from 1865 to 1925.* Norman: University of Oklahoma Press, 1930.

Demos, John. *A Little Commonwealth: Family Life in Plymouth Colony.* New York: Oxford University Press, 1970.

Diamond, Sigmund. *The Reputation of the American Businessman.* Cambridge: Harvard University Press, 1955.

Dickens, Charles. *American Notes.* New York: Wilson & Co., 1842.

Driver, Harold E. *Indians of North America.* Chicago: University of Chicago Press, 1969.

Dusenberry, William H. *The Mexican Mesta: The Administration of Ranching in Colonial Mexico.* Urbana: University of Illinois Press, 1963.

119

Dykstra, Robert. *The Cattle Towns.* New York: Alfred A. Knopf, 1968.

Elson, Ruth. *Guardians of Tradition: American Schoolbooks of the Nineteenth Century.* Lincoln: University of Nebraska Press, 1964.

Erikson, Erik. *Childhood and Society.* New York: W. W. Norton & Co., 1950.

———. *Identity, Youth and Crisis.* New York: W. W. Norton & Co., 1968.

———. *Youth: Change and Challenge.* New York: Basic Books, 1963.

Farb, Peter. *Man's Rise to Civilization as Shown by the Indians of North America.* New York: Dutton, 1968.

Fisher, Marvin. *Workshops in the Wilderness: The European Response to American Industrialization, 1830–1860.* New York: Oxford University Press, 1967.

Fite, Gilbert. *The Farmer's Frontier, 1865–1900.* New York: Holt, Rinehart & Winston, 1966.

Fletcher, Robert H. *From Grass to Fences: The Montana Range Cattle Story.* New York: University Publishers, 1960.

Flower, George. *History of the English Settlement in Edwards County, Illinois.* 1882. New York: Arno Press, 1976.

Frantz, Joe B. *Gail Borden, Dairyman to a Nation.* Norman: University of Oklahoma Press, 1951.

Freud, Sigmund. *Civilization and its Discontents.* Edited and translated by James Strachey. New York: W. W. Norton & Co., 1961.

———. *The Ego and the Id.* Translated by James Strachey. New York: W. W. Norton & Co., 1962.

———. *Inhibitions, Symptoms and Anxiety.* London: International Psycho-Analytical Library, 1936.

———. *Three Essays on the Theory of Sexuality.* 4th ed. Translated by James Strachey. London: Imago Publishing Co., 1949.

Frink, Maurice. *Cow Country Cavalcade: Eighty Years of the Wyoming Stock Growers' Association.* Denver: Old West Publishing Co., 1954.

Frink, Maurice et al. *When Grass was King: Contribution to the Western Cattle Industry Study.* Boulder: University of Colorado Press, 1956.

Fromm, Erich. *Escape from Freedom.* New York: Farrar & Rinehart, 1941.

––––––. *Man for Himself: An Inquiry into the Psychology of Ethics.* New York: Farrar & Rinehart, 1947.

Gard, Wayne. *The Chisholm Trail.* Norman: University of Oklahoma Press, 1954.

Gates, Paul. *The Farmer's Age: Agriculture 1815–1860.* New York: Holt, Rinehart and Winston, 1960.

Glover, Richard. *David Thompson's Narrative, 1784–1812.* Toronto: Champlain Society, 1962.

Goodwyn, Lawrence. *The Democratic Promise: The Populist Moment in America.* New York: Oxford University Press, 1976.

Gracy, David B. II. *Littlefield Lands: Colonization on the Texas Plains, 1919–1920.* Austin: University of Texas Press, 1968.

Gras, N. S. B. *Business and Capitalism: An Introduction to Business History.* New York: F. S. Crofts & Co., 1939.

Gray, Lewis. *History of Agriculture in the Southern United States to 1860.* Washington, D.C.: Carnegie Institution of Washington, 1933.

Greever, William S. *The Bonanza West: The Story of the Western Rushes, 1848–1900.* Norman: University of Oklahoma Press, 1963.

Gressley, Gene M. *Bankers and Cattlemen.* New York: Alfred A. Knopf, 1966.

Greven, Philip J. *Four Generations: Population, Land and Family in Andover, Massachusetts.* Ithaca, N.Y.: Cornell University Press, 1970.

121

Hafen, Leroy. *The Mountain Men and the Fur Trade of the Far West.* 10 vols. Glendale, Calif.: Arthur H. Clark & Co., 1965–72.

Haley, J. Evetts. *Charles Goodnight: Cowman and Plainsman.* Boston: Houghton Mifflin Co., 1936.

———. *George Littlefield, Texan.* Norman: University of Oklahoma Press, 1954.

Hammond, Bray. *Banks and Politics in America from the Revolution to the Civil War.* Princeton: Princeton University Press, 1967.

Heckscher, Eli. *Mercantilism.* Edited by E. F. Soderlund. Translated by Mendel Shapiro. 2 vols. New York: Macmillan Co., 1955.

Heimert, Alan. *Religion and the American Mind: From the Great Awakening to the Revolution.* Cambridge: Harvard University Press, 1966.

Henlein, Paul. *The Cattle Kingdom in the Ohio Valley.* Lexington: University of Kentucky Press, 1958.

Hicks, John D. *The Populist Revolt: A History of the Farmer's Alliance and the People's Party.* Lincoln: University of Nebraska Press, 1961.

Hofstadter, Richard. *The American Political Tradition and the Men Who Made It.* New York: Alfred A. Knopf, 1948.

Holden, William C. *The Spur Ranch: A Study of the Inclosed Ranch Phase of the Cattle Industry in Texas.* Boston: Christopher Publishing House, 1934.

Hornaday, William T. *The Extermination of the American Bison with a Sketch of its Discovery and Life History,* Washington, D.C.: U.S. National Museum Annual Report, 1889.

Horsman, Reginald. *Expansion and the American Indian Policy, 1783–1812.* East Lansing: Michigan State University Press, 1967.

Hurst, James Willard. *Law and the Conditions of Freedom*

in the Nineteenth Century United States. Madison: University of Wisconsin Press, 1956.

Hyde, George E. *Indians of the High Plains: From the Prehistoric Period to the Coming of Europeans.* Norman: University of Oklahoma Press, 1959.

Innis, H. A. *The Fur Trade in Canada.* New Haven: Yale University Press, 1930.

Irving, Washington. *Astoria.* 2 vols. Philadelphia: Carey, Lea & Blanchard, 1836.

Jackson, W. Turrentine. *The Enterprising Scot: Investors in the American West after 1873.* Edinburgh, Scotland: Edinburgh University Press, 1968.

Jefferson, Thomas. *The Papers of Thomas Jefferson.* Edited by Julian P. Boyd. 18 vols. Princeton: Princeton University Press, 1950–71.

Kardiner, Abram. *The Individual and His Society: The Psychodynamics of Primitive Social Organization.* New York: Columbia University Press, 1939.

————, et al. *The Psychological Frontiers of Society.* New York: Columbia University Press, 1945.

Kennerly, William Clark [as told to Elizabeth Russell]. *Persimmon Hill: A Narrative of Old St. Louis and the Far West.* Norman: University of Oklahoma Press, 1948.

King, Peter. *The Development of the English Economy to 1750.* London: Macdonald & Evans, 1971.

Kirkland, Caroline [Mary Clavers]. *A New Home, Who'll Follow? Glimpses of Western Life.* Edited by William S. Osborne. New Haven: Yale University Press, 1965.

Kirkland, Edward C. *Dream and Thought in the Business Community.* Ithaca, N.Y.: Cornell University Press, 1955.

Kluckholm, Clyde and Murray, Henry A., eds. *Personality in Nature, Society, and Culture.* New York: Alfred A. Knopf, 1949.

Kroeber, A. L. *Anthropology, Race, Language, Culture,*

Psychology, Prehistory. New York: Harcourt, Brace & Co., 1948.

Lamar, Howard R. *The Trader on the American Frontier: Myth's Victim.* College Station: Texas A & M University Press, 1977.

Larson, T. A. *History of Wyoming.* Lincoln: University of Nebraska Press, 1965.

Lavender, David. *The Fist in the Wilderness.* Garden City: Doubleday, 1964.

Lawson, Murray. *Fur: A Study in English Mercantilism, 1700–1775.* University of Toronto Studies in History and Economics, no. 9. Toronto: University of Toronto Press, 1943.

Lea, Tom. *The King Ranch.* 2 vols., Boston: Little, Brown & Co., 1957.

Lee, Bob and Williams, Dick. *Last Grass Frontier: The South Dakota Stock Grower Heritage.* Sturgis, S.D.: Black Hills Publishers, 1964.

Lerner, Daniel. *The Policy Sciences: Recent Developments in Scope and Method.* Stanford, Calif.: Stanford University Press, 1951.

Linton, Ralph. *The Cultural Background of Personality.* New York: Appleton-Century-Crofts, 1945.

Lipset, Seymour Martin, and Lowenthal, Leo, eds. *Culture and Society: The Work of David Riesman Reviewed.* Glencoe, Ill.: Free Press, 1961.

Lively, Jack. *The Social and Political Thought of Alexis de Toqueville.* Oxford: Clarendon Press, 1962.

Lockridge, Kenneth. *A New England Town: The First Hundred Years, Dedham, Massachusetts, 1636–1736.* New York: W. W. Norton & Co., 1970.

McCloskey, Robert. *American Conservatism in the Age of Enterprise.* Cambridge: Harvard University Press, 1951.

McCoy, Joseph G. *Historic Sketches of the Cattle Trade of*

124

the West and Southwest. Kansas City, Mo.: Ramsey, Millett & Hudson, 1874.

MacDonald, James. *Food from the Far West . . .* London and Edinburgh: W. P. Nimme, 1878.

McHugh, Tom. *The Time of the Buffalo.* New York: Alfred A. Knopf, 1972.

MacKenzie, Cecil W. *Donald MacKenzie: King of the Northwest.* Los Angeles: I. Deach, Jr., 1937.

Malin, James C. *The Grassland of North America: Prolegomena to Its History, with Addenda and Postscript.* Lawrence, Kansas: James C. Malin, 1947.

Malinowski, Bronislaw. *A Scientific Theory of Culture.* Chapel Hill: University of North Carolina Press, 1944.

Martineau, Harriet. *Society in America.* 2 vols. London: Saunders & Otley, 1837.

Mead, Margaret. *And Keep Your Powder Dry.* New York: William Morrow & Co., 1942.

Mead, Sidney. *The Lively Experiment: The Shaping of Christianity in America.* New York: Harper & Row, 1963.

Merk, Frederick, ed. *Fur Trade and Empire: George L. Simpson's Journal.* 2d ed. Cambridge: Harvard University Press, 1968.

Mesick, Jane Louise. *The English Traveller in America, 1785–1835.* New York: Columbia University Press, 1922.

Meyers, Marvin. *Jacksonian Persuasion: Politics and Beliefs.* Stanford, Calif.: Stanford University Press, 1957.

Miller, David H. and Steffen, Jerome O., eds. *Frontiers: A Comparative Approach.* Norman: University of Oklahoma Press, 1977.

Mikesell, Marvin W. and Wagner, Philip L., eds. *Readings in Cultural Geography.* Chicago: University of Chicago Press, 1962.

Monaghan, Jay. *Australians and the Gold Rush.* Berkeley: University of California Press, 1966.

Morrell, W. P. *The Gold Rushes.* New York: Macmillan Co., 1941.

Mothershead, Harmon R. *The Swan Land and Cattle Company, LTD.* Norman: University of Oklahoma Press, 1971.

Nevins, Allan, ed. *America Through British Eyes.* New York: Oxford University Press, 1948.

Nordyke, Lewis. *Cattle Empire: The Fabulous History of the 3,000,000 Acre XIT.* New York: William Morrow & Co., 1949.

———. *The Great Roundup: The Story of Texas and Southwestern Cattlemen.* New York: William Morrow & Co., 1955.

Oglesby, Richard. *Manuel Lisa and the Opening of the Missouri Fur Trade.* Norman: University of Oklahoma Press, 1963.

Oliphant, Mary C. Simms et al, eds. *The Letters of William Gilmore Simms.* 2 vols. Columbia, S.C.: State Co., 1955.

Oliphant, J. Orin. *On the Cattle Ranges of the Oregon Country.* Seattle: University of Washington Press, 1968.

Osgood, Ernest. *The Day of the Cattlemen.* Minneapolis: University of Minnesota Press, 1929.

Paul, Rodman. *Mining Frontiers of the Far West, 1848–1880.* New York: Holt Rinehart & Winston, 1963.

Peake, Ora. *The American Factory System, 1795–1822.* Denver: Sage Books, 1954.

———. *The Colorado Range Cattle Industry.* Glendale, Calif.: Arthur H. Clark & Co., 1937.

Pearce, W. M. *The Matador Land and Cattle Company.* Norman: University of Oklahoma Press, 1964.

Peck, John. *A Guide for Emigrants, Containing Sketches of Illinois, Missouri, and the Adjacent Parts.* 1831. Edited by Jerome O. Steffen. New York: Arno Press, 1975.

Pelzer, Lewis. *The Cattlemen's Frontier: A Record of the*

Trans-Mississippi Cattle Industry, 1850–1890. Glendale, Calif.: Arthur H. Clark & Co., 1936.

Pessen, Edward. *Jacksonian America: Society, Personality, and Politics.* Homewood, Ill.: Dorsey Press, 1969.

Phillips, Paul. *History of the American Fur Trade.* Norman: University of Oklahoma Press, 1961.

Pierson, George W. *Tocqueville and Beaumont in America.* New York: Oxford University Press, 1938.

Porter, Kenneth W. *John Jacob Astor: Business Man.* 2 vols. Cambridge: Harvard University Press, 1931.

Potter, David M. *People of Plenty: Economic Abundance and American Character.* Chicago: University of Chicago Press, 1954.

Prucha, Francis Paul. *American Indian Policy in the Formative Years: The Indian Trade and Intercourse Acts, 1790–1834.* Cambridge: Harvard University Press, 1962.

Remini, Robert. *Andrew Jackson and the Bank War: A Study in the Growth of Presidential Power.* New York: W. W. Norton & Co., 1967.

Rich, E. E. *Hudson's Bay Company, 1607–1870.* 3 vols. New York: Macmillan Co., 1958–62.

Rickard, Thomas A. *A History of American Mining.* New York: McGraw-Hill, 1932.

Riesman, David. *The Lonely Crowd: A Study of Changing American Character.* New Haven: Yale University Press, 1950.

Rollins, Phillip Ashton. *The Discovery of the Oregon Trail: Robert Stuart's Narratives.* New York: Charles Scribner's Sons, 1935.

Rouse, John E. *Cattle of North America.* World Cattle, vol. 3. Norman: University of Oklahoma Press, 1973.

Saloutos, Theodore. *Farmer Movements in the South.* Berkeley: University of California Press, 1960.

Savage, William W., Jr. *The Cherokee Strip Live Stock Association: Federal Regulation and the Cattleman's Last Frontier.* Columbia: University of Missouri Press, 1973.

——, ed. *Cowboy Life: Reconstructing an American Myth.* Norman: University of Oklahoma Press, 1975.

Schaff, Philip. *America: A Sketch of its Political, Social and Religious Character.* Edited by Perry Miller. Cambridge: Harvard University Press, 1961.

Schmoller, G. *The Mercantile System and its Historical Significance.* New York: Peter Smith, 1931.

Shannon, Fred A. *An Appraisal of Walter Prescott Webb's The Great Plains: A Study in Institutions and Environment.* New York: Social Science Research Council, 1940.

——. *The Farmer's Last Frontier.* New York: Farrar and Rinehart, 1945.

Sheehan, Bernard W. *Seeds of Extinction: Jeffersonian Philanthropy and the American Indian.* New York: W. W. Norton and Co., 1973.

Sheffy, Lester F. *The Francklyn Land and Cattle Company, A Panhandle Enterprise, 1882–1957.* Austin: University of Texas Press, 1963.

Shinn, Charles. *Mining Camps: A Study in American Frontier Government.* New York: Charles Scribner's Sons, 1814.

Simms, William Gilmore. *Guy Rivers: A Tale of Georgia . . .* 2 vols. New York: Lovell, Conyell and Co., 1834.

Skaggs, Jimmy M. *The Cattle Trailing Industry: Between Supply and Demand, 1866–1890.* Lawrence: University of Kansas Press, 1973.

Smith, Duane A. *Rocky Mountain Mining Camps: The Urban Frontier.* Bloomington: Indiana University Press, 1967.

Spence, Clark. *British Investment and the American Mining Frontier, 1860–1901.* Ithaca, N.Y.: Cornell University Press, 1958.

————. *Mining Engineers & the American West: The Lace-Boot Brigade, 1849–1933.* New Haven: Yale University Press, 1970.

Stanton, Alfred H. and Perry, Stewart E., eds. *Personality and Political Crisis: New Perspectives from Social Science and Psychiatry for the Study of War and Politics.* Glencoe, Ill.: Free Press, 1951.

Steffen, Jerome O. *William Clark: Jeffersonian Man on the Frontier.* Norman: University of Oklahoma Press, 1977.

Stephens, A. Ray. *The Taft Ranch: A Texas Principality.* Austin: University of Texas Press, 1964.

Steward, Julian. *Theory of Culture Change: The Methodology of Multilinear Evolution.* Urbana: University of Illinois Press, 1955.

Supple, Barry. *Commercial Crisis and Change in England, 1600–1642: A Study in the Instability of a Mercantile Economy,* Cambridge: At the University Press, 1959.

Sullivan, Dulcie. *The LS Brand: The Story of a Texas Panhandle Ranch.* Austin: University of Texas Press, 1968.

Taylor, Virginia H. *The Franco-Texan Land Company.* Austin: University of Texas Press, 1969.

Thomas, William L., Jr., ed. *Man's Role in Changing the Face of the Earth.* Chicago: University of Chicago Press, 1956.

Thwaites, Reuben Gold, ed. *Original Journals of the Lewis and Clark Expedition, 1804–1806.* 9 vols. New York: Dodd, Mead and Co., 1959.

Tocqueville, Alexis de. *Democracy in America.* Edited by Philip Bradley. New York: Vintage Press, 1945.

Towne, Charles Wayland and Wentworth, Edward Norris. *Cattle and Men.* Norman: University of Oklahoma Press, 1955.

Trimble, William J. *The Mining Advance into the Inland Empire* . . . University of Wisconsin History Series, bulletin 638; vol. 3 no. 2. Madison, 1914.

Trollope, Frances. *Domestic Manners of the Americans.* New York: Dodd, Mead and Co., 1894.

Von Richtofen, Walter, Baron. *Cattle Raising on the Plains of North America.* New York: D. Appleton-Century Co., 1885.

Ward, John William. *Andrew Jackson: Symbol for an Age.* New York: Oxford University Press, 1955.

Webb, Walter Prescott. *The Great Frontier.* Boston: Houghton Mifflin Co., 1952.

White, Leslie. *The Science of Culture.* New York: Farrar, Straus and Cudahy, 1949.

Wilson, Charles H. *England's Apprenticeship, 1603–1763.* New York: St. Martin's Press, 1965.

———. *Mercantilism.* London: Routledge & Kegan Paul, 1958.

Wissler, Clark. *North American Indians of the Plains.* New York: American Museum of Natural History, 1912.

Wood, Gordon. *The Creation of the American Republic, 1776–1787.* Chapel Hill: University of North Carolina Press, 1969.

Wyllie, Irvin. *Self-Made Man in America.* New Brunswick, N.J.: Rutgers University Press, 1954.

Young, Otis. *How They Dug Gold: An Informal History of Frontier Prospecting, Placering, Lode-Mining and Milling in Arizona and the Southwest.* Tucson: University of Arizona Press, 1967.

Zetterbaum, Marvin. *Tocqueville and the Problem of Democracy.* Stanford, Calif.: Stanford University Press, 1966.

ARTICLES

Bailyn, Bernard. "Political Experience and Enlightenment Ideals." *American Historical Review* 67 (January, 1962): 351.

Bircha, K. D. "The Conservative Populists: A Hypothesis." *Agricultural History* 47 (January 1973): 9–24.

Briggs, Harold E. "The Development and Decline of Open Range Ranching in the Northwest." *Mississippi Valley Historical Review* 20 (March 1934): 521–36.

Bryan, T. Conn. "The Gold Rush in Georgia." *Georgia Review* 9 (Winter 1955): 398–404.

Carter, Harvey Lewis and Spencer, Marcia Carpenter. "Stereotypes of the Mountain Man." *Western Historical Quarterly* 6 (January 1975): 17–32.

Chandler, Alfred D. "The Beginnings of 'Big Business' in American Industry." *Business History Review* 33 (Spring 1959): 1–31.

Davis, David Brion. "Ten Gallon Hero." *American Quarterly* 6 (Summer 1954): 111–25.

Davis, K. G. "From Competition to Union." *Minnesota History* 40 (Winter 1966): 166–77.

Davis, W. N., Jr. "Will the West Survive as a Field in American History." *Mississippi Valley Historical Review* 50 (March 1964): 672–85.

Drescher, Seymour. "Toqueville's Two Democracies." *Journal of the History of Ideas* 25 (April-June 1964): 201–16.

Elliott, T. C. "Wilson Price Hunt, 1723–1842." *Oregon Historical Quarterly* 32 (1913): 130–34.

Elkins, Stanley and McKitrick, Eric. "A Meaning for Turner's Frontier: Part I, Democracy in the Old Northwest." *Political Science Quarterly* 69 (September 1954): 321–53.

Elson, Ruth. "American Schoolbooks and 'Culture' in the Nineteenth Century." *Mississippi Valley Historical Review* 46 (December 1959): 411–34.

Erikson, Erik. "Youth: Fidelity and Diversity." *Daedalus: Journal of the American Academy of Arts and Sciences* 91 (Winter 1962): 5–27.

Evans, E. Estyn. "The Ecology of Peasant Life in Western Europe." In *Man's Role in Changing the Face of the Earth,* edited by William L. Thomas, Jr., pp. 217–39. Chicago: University of Chicago Press, 1956.

Faulk, Odie B. "Ranching in Spanish Texas." *Hispanic American Review* 45 (May 1965): 257–66.

Gargean, Edward T. "Toqueville and the Problem of Historical Prognosis." *American Historical Review* 68 (January 1963): 332–35.

Galbraith, John S. "British American Competition in the Border Trade of the 1820's." *Minnesota History* 40 (Winter 1960): 241–49.

Gill, Larry. "From Butcher to Beef King, Conrad Kohrs." In *Cowboys and Cattlemen,* edited by Michael S. Kennedy, pp. 41–58. New York: Hastings House, 1964.

Gladwin, Thomas. "Personality Structure in the Plains." *Anthropological Quarterly* 30 (January 1957): 111–24.

Goetzmann, William H. "The Mountain Man as Jacksonian Man." *American Quarterly* 15 (Fall 1963): 402–15.

Gracy, David B. II. "George Washington Littlefield: Portrait of a Cattleman." *Southwestern Historical Quarterly* 68 (October 1964): 237–39.

Graham, Richard. "The Investment Boom in British-Texas Cattle Companies, 1800–1885." *Business History Review* 34 (Winter 1960): 421–45.

Green, Fletcher. "Georgia's Forgotten Industry: Gold." *Georgia Historical Quarterly* 19, part 1 (June 1935): 94–111; part 2 (September 1935): 201–28.

Gressley, Gene M. "Broker to the British: Francis Smith and Company." *Southwestern Historical Quarterly* 71 (July 1967): 7–25.

Henlein, Paul. "Early Cattle Ranches of the Ohio Valley." *Agricultural History* 15 (July 1961): 150–54.

Horsman, Reginald. "American Indian Policy and the Origins of Manifest Destiny." *University of Birmingham Historical Journal* 11 (December 1968): 128–40.

————. "Indian Policy in the Northwest." *William and Mary Quarterly* 18 (January 1961): 35–53.

Hudson, John. "Theory and Methodology in Comparative Frontier Studies." In *Frontiers: A Comparative Approach,* edited by David H. Miller and Jerome O. Steffen, pp. 11–31. Norman: University of Oklahoma Press, 1977.

Jackson, W. Turrentine. "The Wyoming Stock Growers' Association: Its Years of Temporary Decline, 1886–1890." *Agricultural History* 22 (October 1948): 260–70.

————. "The Wyoming Stock Growers' Association: Political Power in Wyoming Territory, 1837–1890." *Mississippi Valley Historical Review* 33 (March 1947): 571–94.

Jordan, Terry G. "The Origin of Anglo-American Cattle Ranching in Texas: A Documentation of Diffusion from the Lower South." *Economic Geography* 45 (January 1969): 63–87.

Metzger, Walter. "Generalizations about National Character: An Analytical Essay." In *Generalization in the Writing of History,* edited by Louis Gottschalk, pp. 77–102. Chicago: University of Chicago Press, 1963.

Mikesell, Marvin W. "Comparative Studies in Frontier History." *Annals, Association of American Geographers* 51 (1961): 62–74.

Meyers, Sandra L. "The Ranching Frontier: Spanish Institutional Backgrounds of the Plains Cattle Industry." In *Essays on the American West,* edited by Harold M. Hollingsworth, pp. 19–39. Austin: University of Texas Press, 1969.

Nielsen, Jean C. "Donald McKenzie in the Snake Country Fur Trade, 1816–18." *Pacific Northwest Quarterly* 31 (April 1940): 161–79.

Pfiefer, Gottfried. "The Quality of Land Use of Tropical Cultivators." In *Man's Role in Changing the Face of the Earth,* edited by William L. Thomas, Jr., pp. 240–77. Chicago: University of Chicago Press, 1956.

Riesman, David. "From Morality to Morale." In *Personality and Political Crisis: New Perspectives from Social Science and Psychiatry for the Study of War and Politics,* edited by Alfred H. Stanton and Stewart E. Perry, pp. 81–120. Glencoe, Ill.: Free Press. 1951.

————. "Psychological Types and National Character." *American Quarterly* 5 (Winter 1953): 325–43.

Ruckman, J. Ward. "Ramsay Crooks and the Fur Trade of the Northwest." *Minnesota History* 7 (March 1926): 18–31.

Saloutos, Theodore. "The Agricultural Problem of the Late Nineteenth Century." *Agricultural History* 22 (March 1948): 156–74.

Savage, William W., Jr. "The Cowboy Myth." In *The Cowboy: Six Shooters, Songs and Sex,* edited by Charles W. Harris and Buck Rainey, pp. 154–63. Norman: University of Oklahoma Press, 1976.

————. "Plunkett of the EK: Irish Notes on the Wyoming Cattle Industry in the 1880s." *Annals of Wyoming* 43 (Fall 1971): 205–14.

Schmidt, Louis Bernard. "Internal Commerce and the Development of National Economy before 1860." *The Journal of Political Economy* 47 (August 1939): 798–822.

Sorre, Max. "The Concept of *Genre De Vie.*" In *Readings in Cultural Geography,* edited by Marvin W. Mikesell and Philip L. Wagner, pp. 399–415. Chicago: University of Chicago Press, 1962.

Spoehr, Alexander. "Cultural Differences in the Interpretations of Natural Resources." In *Man's Role in Changing the Face of the Earth,* edited by William L. Thomas, Jr., pp. 93–102. Chicago: University of Chicago Press, 1956.

Turner, Frederick Jackson. "The Significance of the Frontier in American History." *American Historical Association, Annual Report for the Year 1893,* pp. 199–227.

Turner, Frederick Jackson. "The West and American Ideals." *Washington Historical Quarterly* 5 (October 1914): 243–57.

Webb, Walter Prescott. "The Western World Frontier." In *The Frontier in Perspective,* edited by Walker Wyman and Clifton B. Kroeber. Madison: University of Wisconsin Press, 1965.

Wesley, Edgar. "The Government Factory System Among the Indians, 1795–1822." *Journal of Economics and Business History* 4 (May 1932): 487–511.

Whittlesey, Derwent. "Major Agricultural Regions of the Earth." In *Readings in Cultural Geography,* edited by Marvin W. Mikesell and Philip L. Wagner, pp. 416–44. Chicago: University of Chicago Press, 1962.

Williams, William Appleman. "The Age of Mercantilism: An Interpretation of the American Political Economy, 1763–1828." *William and Mary Quarterly* 15 (October 1958): 419–37.

Young, Otis. "The Spanish Tradition in Gold and Silver Mining." *Arizona and the West* 7 (Winter 1965): 299–314.

THESES AND DISSERTATIONS

Goble, Danney. "A New Kind of State: Settlement and State Making in Oklahoma to 1907." Ph.D. dissertation, University of Missouri, 1976.

McFarlane, Larry A. "Economic Theories Significant in the Rise of the United States Indian Factory System, 1795–1817," Master's thesis, University of Missouri, 1955.

Index

A

Agriculture: Great Plains, x, xvi–xvii, 95–97; trans-Appalachian, xii–xiii; sub-frontier process, 15
Applegate, George: 83–86
Aram, Joseph: 85
Astor, John Jacob: 41–42
Auraria, Georgia: 75–79

B

Borden, Gail: 55–56
Brisbin, James: 66

C

Cattle Industry: business practices, 67–69; colonial, 52–53; Ohio Valley, 53–54; plains, 54–58
Change: fundamental change defined, x–xiii, xviii; modal change defined, x–xi
Cool, Peter: 87
Cornell, George: 82
Crooks, Ramsay: 42 45

D

Daholonga, Georgia: 75–79

E

Eagle, John: 81–82

F

Frontier: cosmopolitan defined, xii–xvii; economics, 21–22; education, 18–19; insular defined, xii–xvii; law, 20–21; religion, 19–20
Fur Trade: business structures, 36–41; national policy, 29–36

G

Georgia gold rush: 74–79
Goodnight, Charles: 62–63

H

Hudson's Bay Company: 32–34
Hunt, Wilson Price: 43–46

I

Iliff, John: 61–62
Indians: factory system, 35–36; plains culture, 92–95

J

Jackson, Andrew: 17–19
Jefferson, Thomas: Indian policy, 33–36; territorial policy, 31–33

K

Kirkland, Caroline: 28
King, Richard: 56, 59–60

L

Lamb, Harvey: 86
Lewis, Thomas: 81–82, 86
Littlefield, George: 60

M

McClellan, Robert: 42–45
McCoy, Joseph: 57
McKenzie, Donald: 43–46
Mercantile Capitalism: xiv, 29–31, 37–38, 64–65
Mercantilism: 29–32, 35
Mining: business and economics, 75–76; social and political structures, 71–73; *see also* Georgia gold rush
Missouri Fur Company: 38–41
Mountain Men: 47–50
Mythology, Western: xvii

N

North West Fur Company: 32, 34, 39, 46

P

Pacific Fur Company: 41, 46
Peck, John: 27
Piper, Edward: 55
Pittman, Amos: 88
Pomeroy, Charles: 83, 85

S

Sedalia Cattle Trail: 56
Shinn, Charles: 72
Swain, William: 86

T

Tocqueville, Alexis de: 12–13, 28
Turner, Frederick Jackson: xiii, xiv, 3–6, 12–14, 25–28, 72

W

Webb, Walter Prescott: xvi, 4–5, 91
Western history: role of social psychology, 7–11; role of sociology, 9–11